March 2009 —

To my dear friend Anne,
long may she remain one.
Love,
Wendy xx

Lakeland in the 1830s

based on the journal of a gentleman traveller

from Isaac Simpson's original manuscript with
additional research and historical content

Wendy M. Stuart

Wendy M. Stuart.

HAYLOFT PUBLISHING LTD.

First published 2009

Hayloft Publishing Ltd, South Stainmore, Kirkby Stephen, Cumbria, CA17 4DJ

tel: 017683 42300
e-mail: books@hayloft.eu
web: www.hayloft.eu

ISBN 1 904524 62 1 - hardback
ISBN 1 904524 61 3 - paperback

A catalogue record for this book is available from the British Library

Printed and bound in the EU

Papers used by Hayloft are natural, recyclable products made from wood grown in sustainable forests.
The manufacturing processes conform to the environmental regulations of the country of origin.

*For my good friend Commander Sergey Paschenko in Sebastipol,
who told me that he had lost his ancestors - so share with me one of mine!*

*A detailed view of the cover photograph showing gentleman travellers crossing
Dunmail Raise with the carriage in the distance working its way up the hill.*

Acknowledgements

I wish to thank and acknowledge the invaluable assistance of many people who have provided me with help and inspiration, all my various friends for their encouragements, and all the establishments who have offered me many interesting historical facts, and permission given for the use of many old photographs. Those I would like to thank include:

E. D. le Cren, Freshwater Biological Station,
                                    Ferry House, Windermere.
City of Liverpool Records Office.
The Lodore Hotel, Keswick.
The late Mr George Pattison of the Windermere Steamboat Museum.
S. J. Macphearson of Cumbria County Council Archives Department.
Jackie Fay, historian, Kendal Library.
Windermere Library.
Kathy Hayhurst, Holme & District Local History Society.
Mr John Finey.
The Mining Museum in Keswick.
Old School Museum, Hawkshead.

My husband Edward Murphy for his tolerance whilst I have worked, my son Tim Stuart Joynson for his invaluable patience and knowledge of computers, my second son Nick Stuart Joynson on historical inclusions, my third son Jerry Stuart Joynson for allowing me to bounce ideas off him weekly, and my fourth and the youngest, Andy Stuart Joynson as back-up to the other three for the same reasons. I must not forget my dear Aunt Melene Barnes (née Simpson) who gave me the manuscript many years ago to do what I wished with it.

Contents

Foreword

This book is, for the most part, a transcription of an original manuscript written by my Great-Great Grandfather Isaac Simpson. Isaac died in 1859, aged 59 years, his wife Mary Jane lasting until 1871. Isaac's grandson Stephen Simpson was born in September 1863, four years after Isaac's death, and although they never met, Stephen knew a great deal about his grandparents. His grandmother, Mary Jane, who had a great influence on his early life, kept the memories of her husband, Isaac, very much alive by talking about him often, until her death in 1871. Similarly, in my early years, Stephen, my own grandfather, also spoke to me at great length about his grandparents, so I feel I am a small part of the story and have a kind of direct link to part of the past. The manuscript is now in my possession.

I grew up in Grandpa Stephen's house, spending most of my childhood years there. Stephen was still a nineteenth century gentleman living in the first half of the twentieth century, so my sister and I were brought up with strict overtones of the Victorian era, including learning to ride, and we were surrounded with the portraits and artefacts of that earlier period of history, some of which had belonged to Isaac. We played with the Georgian and Victorian clothes we found in old chests, which had been saved for well over a century, and imagined that we were girls who lived in those earlier times.

As the older generations passed away, I gradually acquired many of the portraits, old papers, and most of the Victorian trappings of my grandfather, which engendered in me a pressing need to do something to preserve what I had, for future generations - some unique pieces of history. The manuscript is an account of a journey taken in a horse-drawn gig in 1831 around the Lake District, by Isaac Simpson and his friend Yates, in company with three other young men, and he recorded his observations of the trip for the benefit of 'Dear E.', his young son Edmund Simpson. Many journals of this period were written without the benefit of the recipient's full name.

Isaac wrote his journal at the end of each day with a quill pen, and in the Georgian style of language. Although clearly written and well preserved, after about 180 years, the ink has gradually faded. There is an example in this foreword, and the text contains many words which have fallen out of common usage or are obsolete. The transcription therefore has not been an easy or quick task. Initially I copied the book by hand into a notebook of similar size, then afterwards typed it into the computer, checking every word and spelling at each stage and, in doing so, made a glossary of words and meanings which can be found at the end of this book. The obsolete words required research in much older versions of Chambers and Webster's dictionaries for this task, and given the difficulty in deciphering the manuscript, the transcript has taken several years in the making.

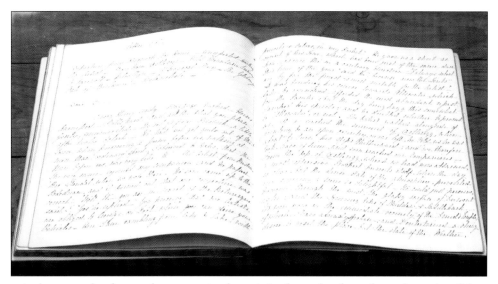

A photograph of a random page in the original notebook to show the style of the quill pen script of the early 1800s.

I also wished to investigate the route of Isaac's journey, and to see the places he wrote about. There has been less building of new roads in Cumbria than elsewhere in England, thus making my task to find them easier; even so, some of the roads have been modernised beyond his recognition. Perhaps the best example is the famously dangerous 'Dunmaile Raise' route to Keswick, which has been straightened, flattened, widened and smoothly surfaced.

Copies of maps made in the 1830s were given to me by Windermere Library to assist me in my task. I searched for the buildings that he visited to see what had survived nearly two centuries, and have visited some of them.

A farm near Ings, unchanged by time. W. M. Stuart, 1992.

Milnthorpe is no longer a seaport. The railway, built only a few years after his visit, cut across the estuary, causing the port for sailing ships to be useless and so it silted up; and the little village of Birthwaite became the final halt to the railway line and the nearest stop to Lake Windermere, three miles from Bowness.

There was no evidence of a date in the manuscript, but it was obviously written in the autumn. I could roughly place this journey in the context of Isaac's life, but this was not sufficient to fix the date. However, the reference to Isaac's visit to Lord Branker's residence, who was away in Liverpool to fulfil his duty as Lord Mayor for that year, confirmed the year of his trip to be the same as the date of Lord Branker's term of office in 1831, the date being recorded in the Mayor's parlour in Liverpool.

There were many choices for the illustrations to this book. I eventually decided to include original etchings, drawn in the early 1800s. These are in keeping with the times, and I have augmented these originals with drawings, paintings and photographs of later dates.

At the outset, I didn't realise that I would be delving into history at such depth, but it has been a pleasure doing so, taking me on a journey into the past, investigating clothes, carriages, customs, and social and industrial history. It has been a mystery tour, prompted by a very personal account of the Lake District in the autumn of 1831, guided by a most 'Academic Gentleman' of the first half of the nineteenth century, who was very much a part of the growing manufacturing industries of his time, and aware of the rapid changes taking place in England.

Wendy M Stuart
Chorley, Lancashire, 2007

A short biography of Isaac Simpson, 1800-1859

Isaac Simpson, 15 September 1800 – 23 March 1859.
A portrait painted in oils by an unknown artist, for Isaac Simpson's wedding,
being a good representation of what he looked like, and the fashions that were in
vogue, at about the time of his journey.

Isaac Simpson wrote a daily journal about a remarkable journey of and in his time, and this book is an account of it. He lived during an age of great industrial expansion. The loss of the American colonies (1776), the ending of the French Revolution (1815), the building of the first railways (1825), the abolition of slavery (1833) and the building of the great cotton mills of Lancashire all added to the excitement of a great new era.

To know more of Isaac, one has to delve into a little of his antecedents. Isaac was a very scholarly young man who was born originally into farming stock, which then became a predominately clock-making and engineering family, so we start briefly with his grandfather, William Simpson, (born 1716), the last of the yeoman farmers of Gisborne in Yorkshire.

William became a turnpike farmer at Slyne (near Lancaster), Greta Bridge, and Heslington. He lived at Greta Bridge and had two sons, John, (1744) who went into the militia, and Stephen Simpson (1752) the first clock-maker in the family, with growing engineering skills. William became a very wealthy farmer who held the leases on several tollgates, or turnpikes in the north west regions, and collected the tolls from the small army of pike-men, (or toll-men) whom he employed. It was a very lucrative business, and the tolls were supposedly to keep the roads in passable order over his stretches of land. So now we touch upon his son Stephen's education, which required money, and William believed a good education would bring wealth.

Stephen Simpson

Stephen Simpson (1752-1821), was apprenticed to a clock-maker in Lancaster. The fee for his apprenticeship was a large one, bordering on £100 (in approximately 1764). Clock-making was a highly skilled and scientific business in those days, and to enable a young man to become efficient at the trade, an immense amount of mathematical study and application was necessary.

It is probable that the word 'clock' originally signified a bell (cloche) with a mechanical appliance to strike it at regular intervals. The manufacture of portable clocks for domestic use began about 1660. The makers had to make all the tools, and the wheels themselves had to be mathematically accurate.

When his apprenticeship, which had included an all round education in mathematics, sciences and the classics, ended, Stephen set up his own business at Greta Bridge, and became a notable clock-maker of his time, as mentioned in Britten's *Old Clocks and their Makers*, fourth edition, 1919.

In 1780, aged 28, Stephen married Elizabeth Porter at the Friends Meeting House in Lancaster. Elizabeth died in 1814. Stephen removed himself and the unmarried members of his family in 1804 to the shop in Preston known as the Tup's Clock, in Cottam Street, at the bottom of Church Street, and continued his blossoming business, which thrived well in that wealthier part of town.

He was an ardent freemason, and became a Freeman of Preston, and a well-known member of Preston society. In 1777 the population of Preston, which was still a small market town, was approximately 12,000, but rapidly increased, because of the cotton trade,

Isaac Simpson's birth certificate.

to well over 24,000 by 1821. In Whittle's *History of the Borough* published in 1821, there were only nine clock-makers in Preston of whom he was the most prominent, and when he died on 24 November 1821 he was a very wealthy man.

Isaac was one of nine children (six sons and three daughters). He was the sixth son of Stephen Simpson, and was born at Greta Bridge on 15 September 1800, but soon moved with his father and family to Preston. The shop of the Tup's Clock, in Cottam Street, where they lived, had affixed to its wall a model of a ram, which used to strike the hours of the day with its horns on a bell.

Stephen held the same views as his father about education, so his six sons became apprenticed in the clock-making trade, requiring a fairly lengthy, expensive and scholarly education, after which they branched out into their own areas of expertise. They took advantage of the growing industrial mills, with the mechanical needs of their day, and put their learning to good use where their skills could earn them a good living, thus becoming 'The Master, not The Man'.

William (born 1781) became a clock and textile machine maker, afterwards making nautical instruments and chronometers in partnership with his son John, the accuracy of which can be found in Kew Observatory records.

Thomas (born 1782) was a machinist and engineer in Horrickses, Miller & Co. cotton mills, making and playing violins in his spare time, and became quite a renowned player.

John (born 1786) the third son was killed at sixteen when a haystack fell on him.

Stephen (born 1791) was a clock-maker, then moved into gas engineering, which led him into inventing the gas mantle, the hydrometer, and erecting many private gas plants for the cotton industry, amongst other things.

Edmond (born 1794) was apprenticed to his father and like him also became a noted clock-maker in Preston.

Isaac (born 1800) the writer of this notebook, and originally a clock-maker.

Isaac was apprenticed to his father and gained a well-rounded education, but also continued his studies by attending night school, and subsequently specialised in pocket chronometers and patent lever watch making. He was twenty years of age when he married Mary Ann Hargraves (1800-1871), in 1820. She was the same age as Isaac. Her father, Robert Hargraves of Skipton, was also a noted clock-maker.

Mary Ann Simpson

Isaac and Mary Ann moved to Market Street, Chorley, a market town nine miles south of Preston, to open a business on his own account, where a watch and jewellery business was still in operation there as late as 1964. Isaac's wife dropped the Ann part of her name for the rest of her life when she discovered that the London to Preston stage-coach was called 'the Mary-Ann.'

Isaac was an ambitious man, and felt that he could make his fortune faster by using his wider knowledge of engineering, rather than from making clocks. In the early 1820s, whilst helping two French women to flatten wire, for weaving into the headings of bolts of cotton cloth, in the Lancashire cotton industry, he could see that there was tremendous scope for advancement with his engineering skills, and invented machinery to draw and flatten wire of all thicknesses for many purposes.

As his business grew, he knew that the way forward could be better achieved in a larger town like Preston, so he moved in November 1831 to Fox Street; thence to Cross Street in 1838, to make room for his expanding numbers of machinery for drawing gold wire; and in 1840 he again moved to Avenham Road to build yet a larger factory, for spinning gold wire, and also encompassing his growing gold thread embroidery and lace-making, a business which was blossoming fast. He patented his inventions in 1853.

He also interested himself in cotton spinning and became joint owner of the Parker Street Spinning Mills in Preston. In 1842 he became joint owner, with his long standing business acquaintance H. W. Johnson, of a long established firm of gold wire drawing and 'Lacemen & Embroiderers' in London, and was admitted into the freedom of the City of London on 5 November 1844.

Isaac bought a piece of land on East Cliff, in Preston, an area which he had often walked upon as a boy, and determined then to make enough money to buy and build a house there. This he did in 1852, naming the new building East Cliff House, a residence used by the family for over fifty years and the house is still there. He had five sons and two daughters.

He died, aged 59, on the 23 March 1859 and was buried in Preston Cemetery, but left a thriving and profitable gold thread works and spinning mills. He was a well-known and well-loved pillar of Preston society, highly

East Cliff House, Preston, 1857.

educated, and, he wrote little passages on many subjects for his children. He was also very religious.

Isaac was always a great problem solver and loved the game of chess, carrying a miniature ivory chess set in his pocket, so that he could find solutions during the evenings. There was an occasion, one Saturday evening, when he became so involved with a friend on a chess problem, "that to the horror of Mr Simpson, a very religious man, the clock struck one on Sunday morning before they were aware of the time" (*Preston Chronicle*, 21 January 1913, describing the introduction of chess in 1840 to the Mechanics Institute, by Mr I. A. Denham)

Isaac and Mary Simpson. Photograph taken in 1852 on the occasion of the completion of East Cliff House.

Isaac's trip to the Lakes in 1831 was partly for business purposes, to look at the Kendal cottons and discuss engineering possibilities, but also to take an unheard-of little holiday. Travelling more than twenty miles from home for most people was rare, for roads were appallingly muddy and rutted, until about 1816 when John McAdam started to create good, smooth, well-drained surfaces, which he experimented with on some of the main routes. Also, the first more detailed maps were being drawn of England, county by county, (following the influence of the maps that were drawn for the Napoleonic wars (1793–1815).

In his diary about his travels through the Lake District, Isaac drew upon his surprisingly well-rounded educational background and wide knowledge, quoting many relevant passages from famous people, with his religious beliefs showing through some of his writing. He wished to share his experiences, so wrote a diary for his son Edmond to read. This has been passed down through the family, was hidden away for a time, and at last came to light again nearly two centuries later.

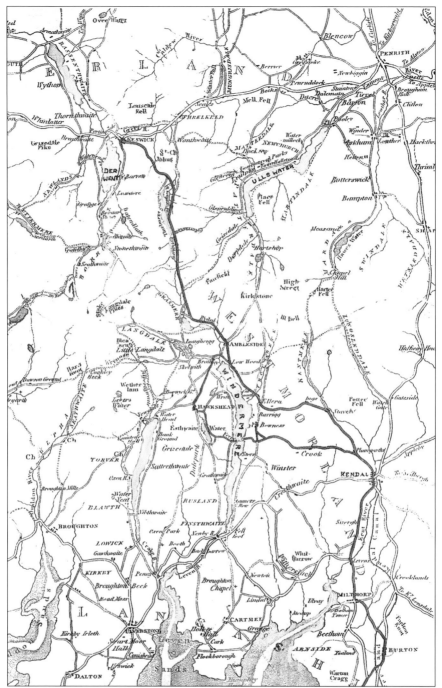

The Lakes, adapted from 'The District of the Lakes' by J. Otley, Keswick, 1818, showing the route Isaac took from Lancaster through the counties of Lancashire, Westmorland and Cumberland to Keswick, situated on the shores of Derwentwater. Isaac passed over Windermere, and by Esthwaite Water, Rydal Water, Grasmere, Wytheburn Mere, Thirlmere, and finally reached Derwentwater.

Letter Contents

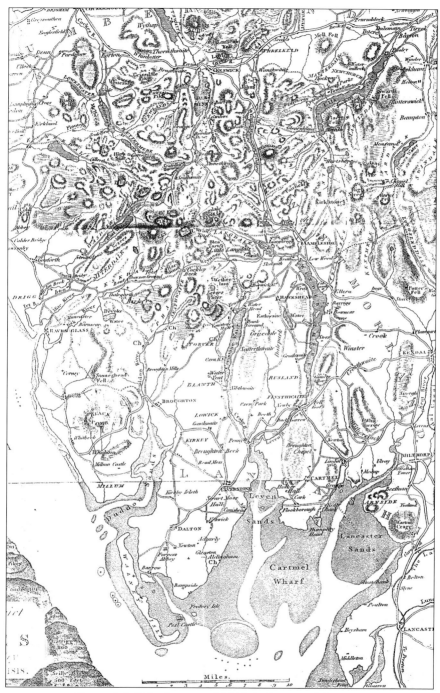

Part of J. Otley's map of 1818 before modification.

Dear E—

Having promised to give you an account
of my late Tour to the Lakes, I now begin to
fulfil that promise, tho' I must confess, at the
outset, that I cannot command Language fitted
to describe the Scenes I have witnessed, in my
short, but interesting, Excursion — I had, indeed
heard and read, much in commendation of
our Lakes: and my Expectations were rather
at a high pitch; but, elevated as they were,
the realities I have seen, have far exceeded
those high Expectations —
My Companions on setting out, were as you are
aware, my Friends Gates & Hamilton —
The commencement of our Tour, was not very
auspicious — The morning, on which I parted
from you, at Preston, you may remember,
was dull, cold, & rainy — This threw a gloom
over our minds — we feared that all our long
anticipated pleasure was about to be blighted —
and we had not proceeded far from Preston,

A Georgian Gentleman's Journal
A journey through the Lakes in 1831

Letter 1

Unpropitious starting; Garstang; brighter prospects; Lancaster; new companions; Burton in Kendal; cottage scene; old maids; Milnthorpe; arrival at Kendal

Dear E...,

Having promised to give you an account of my late tour to the Lakes, I now begin to fulfil that promise, tho' I must confess at the outset, that I cannot command language fitted to describe the scenes I have witnessed in my short but interesting Excursion. I had, indeed, heard and read much in commenda-

Preston looking north from Penwortham Hill, 1829, illustration by J. Harwood.

tion of our lakes; and my expectations were rather at a high pitch; but elevated as they were, the realities I have seen have far exceeded those high expectations.

My companions, on setting out, were as you are aware, my friends Yates and Hamilton; the commencement of our tour was not very auspicious, for the morning on which I parted from you at Preston, you may remember, was dull, cold and rainy. This threw a gloom over our minds. We feared that all our long anticipated pleasure was about to be blighted, and we had not proceeded far from Preston, when it even became a subject of deliberation

We proceeded to Lancaster in better spirits. W. M. Stuart, 1990.

whether we should proceed or return. 'Perseverance' however carried the point, and onward we advanced, securing ourselves as well as we could from the cold, by topcoats and umbrellas of which we had a plentiful supply.

It was well that we proceeded, for more favourable weather we could not have had, and a longer continuance of sunshine had not been witnessed (in this part of the country at least) for several months before, than we had during our week's excursion.

It ceased to rain ere we reached Garstang, and before we arrived at Lancaster the sun's rays began occasionally to break through the hazy atmosphere. We made but a short stay at Garstang to forage the horse, and the occasional glimpse of the sun reviving our hopes of brighter days, we proceeded to Lancaster in better spirits. Here we expected to find Mr. Metcalfe, a friend from Kendal, who had appointed to meet us at eleven o'clock in his gig, to conduct Mr. Hamilton forward to Kendal.

We reached Lancaster about half past twelve. Our Kendal friend had not then arrived, tho' nearly two hours beyond his time. At this we were somewhat disappointed, and as usual in disappointments of this kind, we each of us passed our remarks at the expense of our absent companion.

His letter fixing the time and place of meeting had, unfortunately, been left at Preston, but as Hamilton, to whom it was addressed, was confident that he had not misconstrued it, either in the time or place of rendezvous, our only conclusions were either that Metcalfe was highly culpable in violating his engagement, or that he had met with one of those numerous and unforeseen accidents, to which travellers are ever subjected.

The latter turned out, in sequel, to be the case. Our friend ultimately arrived; in his journey his horse had cast a shoe, and this was the reason for his delay.

I will not detain you long at Lancaster by describing that place. We took a walk on the Castle terrace, and could thence distinctly see the hills of Cumberland and Westmorland, whither we were going.

I had often seen those hills from this place, but never with the same interest as I did at this time. I had theretofore looked at them with comparative indifference, little conceiving what lovely landscapes lay scattered around them. I shall henceforth however, regard those towering hills with sentiments more sublime than heretofore.

Lancaster appeared very dull. The whole town had the appearance of a place deserted by its inhabitants. In our walk we scarcely met a dozen people. Perhaps, however, the town seemed unusually dull to me, who have seldom seen it but during the gaiety and bustle of an assizes.

Having partaken of an excellent dinner at the Royal Oak we left Lancaster about three o'clock, and the afternoon being fair, we had an opportunity of viewing the country as we rode along. On approaching Bolton-le-Sands, a delightful and extensive prospect lay before and around us.

We had on our left a view of Morecambe Bay, with Piel Castle at its entrance. Hest Bank (a small bathing place) stood on the opposite shore with its whitewashed mill and antique looking inn. The bold crags of Wharton and the high hill of Ingleborough stretched themselves on our right, and the hills of Westmorland and Cumberland raised their towering heads in the distance before us.

About half a mile on this side of Burton-in-Kendal there is a mere stone denoting the boundaries of Lancashire and Westmorland; and I cannot pass this stone without remarking that in doing so, I left behind me, for the first time in my life, my native county.

We arrived at Burton (which is a small market town in Westmorland) at about five o'clock. Here, in order to give our horses a little rest we proposed remaining at least half an hour, and as Mr. Medcalfe had some relatives in the immediate neighbourhood of the town, whom he was obliged to call upon, he requested us to accompany him in order, as he observed, that he might the sooner get leave to depart, and we the sooner to get to our journey's end.

We went with our friend, and passing thro' a shady avenue we arrived at the residence of his relatives. It was a neat cottage, the outer walls whereof were covered with evergreens, holly and woodbine, and the patch of ground before the door was scattered with a variety of autumnal flowers. It was indeed a sequestered spot. The inside of the cottage was all neatness and rustic simplicity, and if aught could add to the interest of this rural scene, it was the family, which occupied it.

On our introduction, there sate the matron, an old lady apparently about seventy, and here her daughters, two maiden looking females, the one seemingly about 25, and the other bordering upon 30 years of age. The manners, as well as the dress of the daughters were what we should expect to meet with in the old maid's school; they did not indeed, exhibit the gaiety of dress, and sprightliness of manner of city belles, but they were not, like many of our ancient city belles too often are, dressed in disguise.

The county boundary. W. M. Stuart, 1990.

In our town, and I dare say in

The tea party.   W. M. Stuart, 1995.

yours also, there are some 'antiquated virgins' who, to judge from their dress (without looking at their features) you would take for girls in their teens. It was not so, however, with the Burton maids. No, their dress made them appear far more ancient than their years. They were intelligent, moreover, philosophers forsooth, and when we entered the cottage they were occupied in reading *Daley's Book of Natural and Moral Philosophy.*

After the first salutations were over, we were invited to take tea. We begged to be excused on the grounds that we were anxious to reach Kendal before dark, but all excuses were in vain, all apologies useless. While tea was preparing we strolled into the orchard, and my companions, lacking something to do, in the spirit of juvenile frolic, found an occupation in pelting one another with apples. The sun now began to shed his red rays upon us, which was a warning that we should not longer linger here. We therefore hastened to the cottage to dispose of the good things there provided for us. The young ladies had been actively employed during our short absence, for on our return, the tea was on the table.

A cup of tea is a favourite beverage of mine at all times, but it was particularly so on this occasion, as I had a slight headache, for which tea is generally a cure. I was therefore, upon the whole, glad that we tarried at the cottage, tho' it was at the expense of a little delay on our journey. I was, moreover, pleased with the place.

During our stay at the cottage I was quite 'at home'; Whether or not I manifested on this occasion any extraordinary symptoms of delight I cannot say, but my friend Yates thought so, and he attributed my pleasure to the presence of ladies, more than to any other cause; and he took occasion to whisper in my ear during tea, that Miss—, the younger sister, from her features, habits of study and retirement was, in his opinion, more suitable to my taste, "than any lady he had ever met with."

I cannot say that I agreed with my friend in this opinion, but notwithstanding my dissent, he frequently took occasion, during the further progress of our tour to remind me of the Burton Beauty. The well-buttered teacakes soon disappeared, and we took our leave of this apparently happy family and their sequestered abode, some of us, doubtless, forever. We quickly returned to the inn, and our horses, being refreshed as well as ourselves, we went on at a brisk trot towards Milnthorpe.

It was now twilight, and tho' that medium of vision may suit well to solemn meditations (such as Gray's *In a country churchyard*) yet it is not the

Milnthorpe Sands, Westmorland, 1828. T. Allom.

26

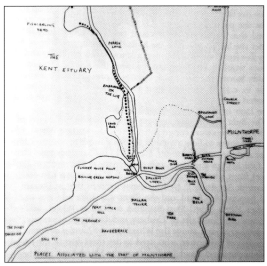

The Port of Milnthorpe.

sort of light fitted for the tourist of pleasure, who is desirous of beholding every object in his way that is worth looking at. Being informed that the scenery about Milnthorpe (it is the only seaport of Westmorland) and thence to Kendal was of a pleasing and varied kind. I regretted much that we had not an opportunity of beholding it.

I had proposed that we should remain at Milnthorpe all night, to enable us to see the scenery the next day, but my companions were desirous of reaching Kendal that evening, (and perhaps there was no wonder at Medcalfe desiring this, for he is a married man) and I therefore did not press my proposal.

At Milnthorpe we took up Mr. Edward Medcalfe, brother of our Kendal friend, and after a ride of a little more than an hour's duration by starlight, we arrived at Kendal about ten o'clock. Yates and I took up our quarters at the Commercial Inn, where we were well accommodated; and Hamilton was offered a bed at Mr. Medcalfe's, at whose house we were invited to supper. I had, however, three reasons for declining the invitation - I was fatigued with my journey, and had a slight headache, and was wishful to be up betimes in the morning. My reasons were readily available, and it was not long after our arrival before I retired to my chamber.

The Commercial Hotel, Kendal, photograph circa 1900.

Letter 2

*Invitation to breakfast with Mr. Medcalfe; his character; antiquity;
Castlelaw Hill; Kendal woollen manufactories;
Kendal Castle and Bowling Green; arrangements*

Dear E...,

The sun had not been long on his journey when I awoke from my slumbers, which had been somewhat disturbed by the pain in my head; and it was with no little pleasure that I saw his Majesty the King of the Day, brilliantly decorated in his Eastern Robes.

I awoke Yates from a sound sleep, and as we had received a pressing invitation to breakfast with Mr. Medcalfe, we soon found ourselves at his house, and were ushered into the breakfast room by his good lady, who had prepared for us a substantial repast. As one of our companions, not having yet risen, and the other, seemed as if he had not had enough of repose, we strongly suspected that both of them had been sitting too long 'looking at each other' the previous evening.

Medcalfe I understood to be a 'jovial soul', 'a hearty good fellow'; indeed, his countenance at first sight indicated to me that such was his character. His features are the very picture of what is the boast of Westmorland – honesty and sincerity; his spirits are of the lively kind, his jokes numerous, but of the homely cast.

He had seen somewhat of the world (for his business leads him much to travel) and he is not therefore, Ignorant of Mankind. His domestic virtues are Prudence and Sobriety; he is peculiarly attentive to his business (a woollen manufacturer) – but although his general habits are sober, yet when in the company of kindred spirits, he sometimes is tempted (as the topers term it) to 'overstep the line.'

Breakfast being over, we sallied forth to see whatever was interesting in the town of Kendal. Kendal Castle, now in ruins, is the principal object of attraction to the stranger. This place is rendered peculiarly interesting as having been

The Main Street, Kendal, Westmorland, 1830.   W. Westall A.R.A.

the birthplace of one of our Queens, Catherine Parr, the last wife of Henry VIII.

There is something in the sight of a ruined castle that is calculated to fill the mind of the beholder with serious thoughts and humiliating reflections; it carries his ideas back far beyond the period of his birth, and makes him regard himself, as he aught, the being of a short existence.

Such a sight speaks volumes to a thinking man. It teaches him that Time, the destroyer of all things, will soon take him away; and that titles, honour and wealth must soon sink in the dust. It teaches him in fine his native nothingness.

I am an ardent lover of Antiquity. Nothing, indeed, gives me greater pleasure than ruminating amidst the relics of ancient days. Having told you this, I need scarcely add that a trip to the castle was by all means to be taken. Before we went thither, however, our friend Medcalfe took us to a high mound, at the west end of the town, called Castlelaw Hill.

Tradition has it that this hill was raised by Cromwell, as a place on which to place his cannon for the battery of the castle; and this tradition I think, is not improbable, for the mound is, from its regularity of shape, evidently an artificial one – it is directly opposite the castle; is of equal elevation with it, and is, moreover, at a favourable distance for Canon Shot.

The hill being very steep, and the pathway being slippery by the late rains, I had scarcely proceeded half way in my ascent, when I came tumbling down on all fours. I was soon on my legs again, and when I reached my companions, who were already at the top, I found them indulging in a hearty laugh at my sudden and involuntary retrogression. On the summit of the hill is an Obelisk, with this inscription upon it, 'Sacred to Liberty', and denoting also that it was erected by the inhabitants of Kendal in commemoration of

Visiting the woollen mills, W. M. Stuart.

the 'Glorious Revolution' of 1688. The sides of the Mound having of late been planted with trees, we had only a partial view of the castle thro' the branches.

Our Kendal friend next conducted us to the manufactories. Kendal, you know, is celebrated for its manufacture of coarse woollens – in these consist its staple trade; and singularly enough, these *Woollens* go by the name of Kendal *Cottons*.

Tho' the Kendalonians boast of the extent of their manufactories, yet to anyone who has seen your Manchester Cotton Mills, the former when compared with the latter, must appear as a pigmy to a giant.

We went through one of the largest of the woollen mills, and it was curious to see the process of manufacture. But the strong, greasy smell, which proceeded from the wool, and the astounding noise of the heavy machinery, was far from rendering a protracted stay here desirable.

We therefore left this noisy place and were proceeding to the castle, when Medcalfe, thinking probably that whatever was connected with his trade, must be interesting to everybody under all circumstances, must needs show us through a manufactory of waistcoat pieces.

He here introduced us to Mr. Crosthwaite, the proprietor of one of these concerns; a young man who, at first look, you would take for modesty itself; but as I shall hereafter have occasion to introduce you more particularly to this gentleman, I shall merely observe at present of his manufactory, that we were highly gratified with what we saw there. The weaving of embroidered waistcoat pieces is a curious process, and very different from any weaving I had before witnessed.

We now approached the castle by a gently sloping ascent, from the top of which is a commanding view of the town and neighbourhood of Kendal. At the foot of the hill flows the River Kent (from which the town takes its name), the stream of which is very rapid, and this rapidity is well calculated for the working of the mills, though it prevents the river from being navigable.

The ruins of the castle, when we reached them, we found much less extensive than they appeared from Castlelaw Hill on the opposite side of the river; they form, in fact, but a mere skeleton. The castle had evidently been surrounded by a deep moat, and on the other side of the moat the remains of a wall are still perceptible. The hill on which this ancient fabric stands is

Kendal Castle, 1825. T. Allom.

31

barren, except on the western side, which has recently been planted with trees.

Part of four towers and the main walls is all that is left of this once strong tower. Under the western bound tower, fronting the town, there is a small gloomy cell, which we concluded had been a place of captivity.

Under the two northern square towers, are seen the remains of vaults, the original extent whereof we could form no idea, as they are now already filled with rubbish. None of the walls, forming the inner work of the castle, are now visible, the whole place in the interior of the building being covered with the greensward; here and there, however, there was a hillock, denoting that there once had been some superstructure on the spot.

It is said that an extensive underground communication has been lately discovered near the castle. In traversing these ruins I could not help carrying my ideas back to the time when the castle was in its splendour. I pictured to myself its situation at the period of the birth of the Royal Catherine; and contrasted its then state with what it now is.

Upon those towers, now dismantled, I fancy I saw the flags of the lordly proprietor, streaming in the air to denote to his surrounding tenantry, the joyous event of an addition to his family. In those vaults, now filled with rubbish, I imagined the portly Butler dealing out his exhilarating beverage, to drink to the health of the illustrious stranger. There in that Gateway, now covered with weeds, my fancy drew the liveried porter, ushering into the presence of his Noble Master, his congratulating visitors. And there:

> *Where a few base walls the Place disclose*
> *The Lofty Hall, and Stately Chamber rose...*

Whilst I was indulging in this train of thought, I unconsciously strayed from my companions, and was brought to a sense of having done so by one of them rather vehemently using the epithets 'beautiful,' 'excellent,' 'fine,' and 'grand.' Being curious to ascertain to what these laudatory adjectives were applied, I made up to my friends and found that Medcalfe was applying these fine sounding names to the Kendal Bowling Green, and that the subject of conversation was a meditated game at bowls, at which you must know, both my companions are adepts.

As the day was now far advanced, and as I wished to reach Bowness in

Great-coats and frock coats in 1829.

good time, I used these reasons as dissuasives from their then trying their skill. But finding they were bent upon a game, I thought the sooner they got to it the better and we therefore left the castle and proceeded to the bowling green. I will not dwell longer upon this expedition than to observe that I was somewhat compensated for the delay it occasioned, by the fine prospect I had from the Green, of the town of Kendal and the country around it with the castle in the distance. And my friend was as amply requited on his part, by the fineness of the green, and the excellence of the play.

The game over, we hastened to the inn to prepare for our departure. Before we left Kendal however, we made the following arrangements as to our future plans and further progress; Hamilton, who was about to pay a visit to his relatives at Carlisle, should return thence to Kendal the following evening (Tuesday), and that he and Messrs. Medcalfe and Crosthwaite should meet Yates and me at Low Wood, on the banks of Windermere, early Wednesday morning, and that we should proceed together to Keswick.

Letter 3

Journey from Kendal to Bowness; distant view of Windermere;
twilight view of the lake from its banks; characters of our fellow guests at
the White Inn; gloomy anticipations; unexpected visit; melody; parting.

Dear E...,

The course of our future journey having been chalked out, as mentioned in my last letter, Yates and I set off from Kendal for Bowness about three o'clock on Monday afternoon. The distance is nine miles; the road is very uneven and plainly indicates to the traveller that he is approaching a mountainous country.

There is nothing interesting on this road. As if to form a striking contrast to the beautiful scenery immediately beyond it, you see nothing but barren rocks and wasteland, with little and few, if any, houses. There is nothing

Bowness and Windermere Lake, Westmorland, 1833. T. Allom.

indeed, to relieve the rugged monotony of the scene, except now and then a view of the distant mountains, amongst which Coniston Old Man, Bowfell and the Langdale Pikes are conspicuous.

Being now about a mile from Bowness, I began to look out for Windermere, for my guidebook told me that the lake was perceptible from about this distance from the village. The lake was soon in sight, and at the first sight I, like a celebrated tourist

The White Lion, Bowness, approximately 1870.

who had gone before me, exultingly cried out, "Windermere!"

I must confess I was somewhat disappointed at the first view of this lake; it appeared little better than the River Ribble. After advancing about half a mile further, however, it appeared much more to advantage, its glassy surface being then seen from betwixt the trees with which the lake is bordered; it had a fine effect. Immediately before us lay the beautiful and romantic village of Bowness, which we concluded to make our resting place for the night.

We drove to the White Lion, (the Head Hotel), an excellent inn, where we secured beds for the evening; having quickly unpacked our luggage, and arranged some little matters at the toilet, we sallied forth to view the Lake of Windermere, being anxious to get a sight of it as soon as we could.

In going to the lake, we passed through a winding avenue in which were several neat cottages, built for the accommodation of visitors and decorated in the most tasty manner. Many of them had rustic porches of latticework, through which the woodbine crept, and besides which the rose blossomed. The cottages thus presented a picturesque appearance, and the walks past them were more like the private walks of a gentleman's pleasure ground than those used in common by the public.

We now reached the banks of Windermere. The sun had just disappeared behind the hill on the opposite shore, and we had not, therefore, the most favourable light for viewing the lake. Indistinct, however, as many of the objects were, we nevertheless saw enough to excite our admiration. The distant mountains, with their 'cloud capped' summits, the numerous islands on the lake with their tufted trees, having the chief of them, Curwen's Island in the middle; the dark blue-wooded hill rising in the distance above Curwen's Isle; the boats at anchor in the several bays, and the surface of the cerulean lake ruffled by a gentle breeze, all combined to render this scene one of the most delightful I had ever seen.

The stillness that prevailed, for not a sound was heard, save the rippling of the water on the margin of the lake, and the solitariness of the scene too, for Yates and I seemed to be the only persons who were then enjoying it, gave to the whole prospect a tinge of melancholy loveliness such as I delight in.

> *Hushed were the rich Autumnal Woods*
> *And silence from the dewy hill,*
> *Looked down on pastoral solitudes,*
> *And breezeless lake – where all was still.*

Turning round the edge of a small bay, we had a view of the head of the

Bowness Bay, 1831. Isaac Simpson

lake, and here I took my pencil and sketched the scene, after which we has-tened to the hotel, highly gratified with what little of the lakes we had already seen, and well prepared to make up for our long fasting by a substantial repast.

On our return to the inn, we found an accession of visitors – an elderly gentleman, without a companion; and two young collegians had taken pos-session of our room. We were not long in finding out that our fellow guests were not of that class in whose company we could spend the evening pleas-antly, for all of them seemed to be of the anti-social order of human beings.

The solitaire did not utter a word, and nor did we, being his juniors, deem it becoming to disturb his taciturnity. With respect to the two coxcomb Cantabs, they thought proper to confine their conversation to themselves, and they ultimately put an end to all chances of forming a conversational party by introducing the backgammon board.

Having a long night before us, I began to be uneasy at the idea of having to spend it in such company. We ordered tea, however, and were determined to take up as much time over that as possible – and in this we did but imitate the example of the collegians that, I thought, would not finish tea until bedtime.

Over this my favourite meal, I began to deliberate as to some expedient to occupy the remainder of the evening. My deliberations, however, were of short duration, for we had not quite finished our tea, when a gig drove up to the hotel and in a minute afterwards, who should enter the room but our Kendal friends, Messrs. Medcalfe and Crosthwaite.

Such a visit was as agreeable as it was unexpected, and it put an end at once to all my cogitations as to the mode of spending the evening, for in such company as that of our Kendal companions, I well knew that time would go unhippingly on.

I have already given you a sketch of the character of Medcalfe, and Crosthwaite was

'A young man of some fortune.'

37

in some aspects like him. He is a young unmarried man of some fortune, is about 25, of handsome features and modest look (as I have said before).

He is a native of Keswick and possesses a little of the Cumberland brogue. He, like Medcalfe, has travelled a great deal, and has thereby acquired some knowledge of the world. Being of rather delicate constitution and abstemious habits, a very little wine has the effect of making him a merry companion, and both he and Medcalfe were in such mood when they arrived at Bowness.

The silence, which had for some time prevailed in the room, was soon disturbed by the entrance of our merry companions, whose first movement was to call for a bottle of wine, as a refresher after their journey. It was soon apparent that the Cantabs and the Solitaire were not the sort of company that suited our newly arrived friends. I caught Medcalfe regarding with a keen eye, the two Cantabs at the opposite side of the room, as much as to say, "I heartily wish there were a partition-wall between us!"

This hint being taken, and we quitted the room, leaving the collegians to their game, and the solitary gentleman to his meditations, nor did we see any of them afterwards. We did not immediately, on leaving the room, adjourn to another, but as Medcalfe was desirous of seeing his horse fed, we went with him to the stable.

It is not uncommon for travellers, when from home, to assume a consequence above their station, and our companion, Crosthwaite, by way of frolic, thought he would try his skill at such dissimulation; he was not long in meeting with a favourable opportunity of doing so. His horse had not been properly attended to, and he peremptorily called for the hostler, demanding of him why he had not done so and so, in such a lordly style, that his chiding would not have discredited an aristocratic tyrant.

I was in pain for the poor fellow, but was subsequently glad to find that Crosthwaite had amply rewarded him, for on mentioning the matter to him after our friends had gone, he said that he, "saw the Gentleman had had too much wine, but he behaved very well," and he, the hostler, "should like to see him again."

Crosthwaite was quite on cue for a little more sport; the village, indeed, did not afford much scope for it, but what little there was, Crosthwaite was anxious to avail himself of it.

He took us to a shopkeeper's, whose signpost denoted him to be a dealer

The village of Bowness, from the Fenty's collection, approximately 1870s.

in almost everything. He was a vendor of fine food and clothing, a man-milliner, draper, grocer and ironmonger. Here Crosthwaite personated a Commercial Traveller, and pressed upon the attention of honest looking Barrow, (for that was the name of the shopkeeper), a certain commodity that was good, cheap and handsome, an 'article' likely to suit the bonny lasses of Bowness.

No persuasives, however, could induce the shopkeeper to give our companion an order; for he said (and he said truly) that he already dealt in numerous articles, and he had no wish to add to this number. We therefore wished him a good night, hoping he would give our friend an order, the next time he solicited him.

We next proceeded to perambulate the village where we scarcely met a single pedestrian; in passing by the church, the spirited youth, Crosthwaite, espying a wheelbarrow in the lane, overhauled it into the churchyard; where I daresay it would remain there unobserved until it attracted the notice of the

Bowness Church, from the Fenty's collection, 1869.

villagers, when the church bell summoned them to their devotions. I gently remonstrated at this act, as being derogatory to that sense of veneration, which we aught to have for so sacred a spot, but Crosthwaite justified the act as a harmless piece of sport.

Being wishful to see what sort of an inn the Crown was, we next went thither, and were much amused, when passing thro' the front apartment, at the sight of a motley group that were there regaling themselves with ale. Here were farmers, hostlers, waiters and village tradesmen, all in merry mood over their ale mugs, sitting around a blazing fire. It was a sort of Harvest Home, and the countenances of all this company indicated that they had, for the present, no 'carking care' to contend with.

Having in our short sally impersonated my Lords in the stable, Commercial Travellers at the shopkeepers, sparks in the village lane and Topers at the Crown, we returned to our headquarters, to finish the remainder of the evening in talking over and commenting on our varied exploits. Many a hearty laugh we had and right merry, I assure you, we were over the last bottle. In the midst of our hilarity, our attention was suddenly arrested by the harmonious strains of instrumental music, which by and by was accompanied by the sweet sounds of a female voice. We listened attentively; it was a lady singing to the piano in an adjoining room. The music was melodious, enchanting and enrapturing. The sounds soon died away, and a deep silence ensued.

The Crown Inn, from the Fenty's collection, approximately 1870s.

It was now near 10 o'clock, and our Kendal friends began to talk of leaving us. The evening was fine, and the moon rode triumphantly in the heavens, which were unshaded by a cloud, so we took our leave of them, under a promise to meet at Low Wood, the day but one after. After partaking of a light supper we retired to rest.

Letter 4

Morning view of the lake of Windermere; High Crag on the east of Bowness; peremptory summons to return to the inn; descent; breakfast; a sail on the lake.

Dear E...,

I have seldom witnessed a more delightful morning than that on which I arose at Bowness. My sleep had been somewhat disturbed, not by indisposition, however, as on the previous night, but by the images of rural cotts and shady groves, beautiful lakes and lofty mountains, flitting across my half-sleeping and half-waking thoughts, yet I arose about six o'clock.

Wasting as little time as possible in my chamber, which overlooked the village and was directly opposite the shop of honest Barrow, I was soon out of doors, and ere Yates made his appearance, I had spent some time on the beautiful grass plot behind the hotel. This plot, being considerably elevated, commands a fine view of the lake and scenery around it.

I was here reclined upon a rustic seat, contemplating the varied objects before me, when the servant brought me a message from my friend that I had got on one of his boots. I suppose I had been in too great a haste to enjoy the morning breeze to pay much attention to the maxim of *Mecum et Tecum*. I had left my own boot, however, in the place of my companion's, and as 'exchange is no robbery,' my conscience was not accused of violating any moral precept. It was a mistake that was soon rectified, and being so, we sallied out without any fixed destination, but to walk just where chance or caprice might lead us.

As we had not hitherto seen the whole extent of Windermere, we bent our course on a high hill or crag on the east of the village, from the top of which we conceived that we should be able to see the whole extent. Though this hill is but a dwarf compared with such as Skiddaw, Saddleback or Helvellyn, yet we considered it of no trifling elevation, I assure you.

After passing up a lane extending about three hundred yards from the village,

Bowness from Belle Isle, Windermere, 1832.   T. Allom.

and through a gate at the extremity, we proceeded in our ascent, at first by a beaten footpath. This track, however, did not reach more than midway to the top, and from its brief termination, one would infer either that the generality of visitors has been satisfied with a half ascent, or they had not dared to advance further. From the steepness of the declivity, the further progress, however, did not appear to us to be attended with any danger, and tho' we had no further tract to guide us, yet we proceeded onward by the best way we could.

Climbing one crag after another, some of which were almost perpendicular, we at length reached the summit. To say we were compensated for the labour we bestowed in this ascent, would not be going far enough. We were more than compensated; we were repaid with usury.

Having seated ourselves upon the very top most crag, the whole country for miles around lay exposed to our view. Behind us was the sterile tract of ground, over which we had travelled the day before, but before us, or rather beneath us, on our right and left, the view was truly grand.

The whole length of Windermere was seen with its numerous bays, and

43

Bowness, facing Windermere, 1842.   J. Harwood.

tufted islands. On the further shore, to our left, the principal object in the landscape was the Station, a small Tower of Observation, with its turret rising from amidst a rich variety of foliage. A little below the Station, stood the Ferry House half covered with trees.

In the midst of the lake, and nearly fronting us, lay Curwen's Island, with its rotund mansion, fine green lawns, and beautiful plantations. Several boats were upon the lake, which gave an increased liveliness to the scene, but they appeared to us at this distance but as so many cygnets.

The village of Bowness was immediately beneath us, forming the foreground of this interesting prospect, and hill rising over hill constituted the extreme perspective – this was truly one of the most magnificent panoramic views I had ever seen.

It is impossible to give you an adequate description of this view. You must see it, to form a just idea of its magnificence. Suffice it to say that it was a luxury indeed to the sight, and we continued gazing upon it with fixed attention until we began to feel that something else than sight required satisfying.

Our fast was yet unbroken, and our stomachs began to experience the effects of the bracing air on the mountain top, which rendered the demand of supplies so imperative that we could no longer resist the call. We cautiously descended from our elevated station, in which operation we were under the necessity of using both hands and legs for walking.

We made the best of our way to the inn, where a blazing fire (a thing unusual in the lakes) quickly set to rights our benumbed limbs; and some excellent coffee with a *quantum sufficit* of eggs soon silenced the craving of our appetites. We concluded over breakfast that our next trip should be upon the lake, and we ordered that the boatman should be in readiness. As soon as we had finished our repast, we walked down to the place of embarkation, a small bay below the Church.

Before I take you along with me upon the lake, it may be as well to give you a general description of it. The lake of Windermere is claimed by the people of Westmorland as theirs, and yet the whole of the western shore and part of its eastern are in Lancashire. This is the largest of the English lakes, its length is near eleven miles, and its average breadth about a mile; tho' in some places it is much wider, and in others scarcely half that width. Its depth is immense; being in some places as much as forty fathoms.

Its waters wash the shores of fourteen islands of various sizes; most of them covered with trees and the lesser of them with brushwood. The chief of these is Belle Isle, or more frequently called Curwen's Island, from its

Bowness Bay from a painting, 1795.

45

belonging to a gentleman of that name who has a handsome house upon it. This island contains about thirty acres of land and is about half a mile in length.

The lake affords fine sport for anglers, abounding as it does in the Finny tribe. Here are found trout, pike, perch, and char, the last of which is a species of fish found only in the deepest waters. There is a little coasting trade in wood, charcoal, and fish carried on upon this lake and the principal port is the village of Bowness.

Our boatman, having arrived with his cushions for the seats, and the boat being hauled to the quay, we were, in a few moments afterwards, upon the limpid water of Windermere. Our guide was 72 years of age, tho' he seemed to be no more than 50. He was of a stout frame, and his countenance bespoke that he had long been engaged in a laborious occupation, for it was indeed weather-beaten.

As our boatman had traversed the lake for thirty years, he had a perfect knowledge of every spot of ground about it, nor was he unwilling to impart

Storrs Hall, from the road to Ulverston, 1832. W. Banks.

Windermere, looking north, from Bowness Bay.   W. M. Stuart.

this knowledge to others, so far from that he was peculiarly communicative.

"There," said he, as we sailed along, "on your right, Gentlemen, towards the head of the lake, is Rydal Head, and sate not far from it is the residence of the late Bishop Watson."

"Yonder", he continued, "on your left, about a mile below, you perceive a handsome building; that is Storrs Hall, the seat of Colonel Bolton."

"There stands Holly Hill, the residence of Mrs Bellases".

"There, the Villa, the seat of Captain Starkie.[1]"

"That is Rayrigg, and there is Belle Grange."

Thus did our loquacious old guide amuse us by describing the various places and objects around us. Our guide's descriptions did not in the least retard our progress, for notwithstanding that he now and then turned his head, to look at the place he was talking of, yet he still rowed on, and plied his oars with astonishing agility. His course was directed towards Curwen's Island,

---

[1] NOTE: Captain Starkie charted Windermere for navigational purposes.

between which, and us, lay a Holme, or Island, which was covered with wood.

In passing this, we had to row through a rough and rapid current. The forecastle of the boat was considerably elevated above the stern, and knowing that this was one of the deepest parts of the lake, and that if the boat were upset, a watery grave would have been inevitable, I confess that I felt rather alarmed in passing through this current. The guide assured us however, that there was no danger. His countenance plainly indicated that he was confident there was none, so we took courage, and soon got clear of the impetuous stream.

We now moved steadily on, and having got rid of the Holme, we had a most enchanting view of the whole lake. Nothing can equal the view of the surrounding scenery from the surface of the water; the numerous islands with their tufted trees; the boats at anchor in the bays with their red pennons floating in the air, and here and there a boat skimming along the surface of the lake.

There were handsome mansions or rustic villas on the banks, as far as the eye could reach with huge mountains rising in the distance.

We viewed the white houses of Bowness with its steeple of the little church half embosomed in trees, and a few coasting vessels plying to and fro. Above us we had a serene sky, beneath us a limpid lake reflecting every object with the utmost fidelity, and around us every variety of the picturesque. Hill and dale, wood and water, mansions, villages, cottages, islands, altogether this constituted a scene, which far surpasses verbal description.

Letter 5

*Approach to Curwen's Island; a new guide; a walk through the isle;
views from it; its proprietor; sail to the ferry; walk to the station;
prospects from the observatory.*

Dear E...,

The view of Curwen's Island, on our next approach to it was exquisitely fine.
Being informed by our aquatic guide that its proprietor was not only willing,
but also wishful that strangers should visit it, we were desirous to avail ourselves of the permission.   Having intimated our wish to the boatman, he
adroitly steered his little bark to the island harbour, where we found a man

The Round House on Belle Isle.   W. M. Stuart, 1987.

49

waiting, who politely handed us to the shore, and offered to conduct us through the grounds.

This person was a servant of Mr. Curwen's, and his office was that of Conservator of the Island. We found him a very loquacious companion; his manners extremely condescending; he had a ready, tho' somewhat lengthy, answer to every enquiry, relative to this insolated spot. His intelligent observations would have been far from discreditable to one in a much higher walk of life, than that of an Island Ranger.

Our guide first conducted us to the northern point of the isle, leaving the house of Mr. Curwen (which is about the middle of it) at our rear. The walks were in excellent order and the foliage of the trees, which overhung them, and fringed the lake, exhibited a thousand different autumnal hues, from the darkest brown to the liveliest green. At one moment we were completely embowered in a grove, and anon, a beautiful view of the lake was visible.

Having turned round the northern point of the island, a new variety of scenery was presented to our view. A high hill, covered with wood, rose from the opposite shore, with pasture and cornfields reaching from the foot of the hill to the verge of the lake. A neat farmhouse too, on the opposite side of the water gave additional interest to the scene. This farm belongs to Mr. Curwen, who keeps all his cattle there, not permitting any to graze on the island.

From the western strand, which we were now traversing, we had some delightful views up the lake, and from our spot in particular, beside a large and ancient oak, there is a charming prospect. At this spot our guide told us that it was a favourite retreat for ladies, as being an eligible situation from which to sketch the surrounding scenery. Time would not permit me to use my pencil here, or I would fain have done so.

The picture would have been as follows – before us the lake, with the blue hills of Rydal and Ambleside, constituting the horizon. On the left, rising majestically, was the wooded mountain I have just now mentioned and at its foot the farmhouse with the verdant lawns and smiling cornfields. The indentations of the island on which we were, with its trees of various forms and hues were to the right. The graceful willow, the stately poplar, the waving ash and the huge oak reached down to the water's edge, and extended to the very spot where we were standing, presenting a beautiful variety of trees.

This is just such a scene, in my opinion, as is calculated to please a female artist, and it would, perhaps, have tended much to increase the interest of this scene, if I could have placed in the foreground a fair female sketching it. That what was not, however, I have ventured to supply by fancy.

The house of Mr. Curwen is of a circular form, as before noticed, and its cupola is seen from various parts of the island rising above the trees. We learned from our conductor that the major part of Mr. Curwen's family had left the island a few days before we were there. Mr. Curwen was still at the house, but intended to leave it shortly to attend the marriage ceremony of one of his daughters, which was about to take place.

He is a man of domestic habits, is fond of books, and having a numerous family, is never at a loss for society. He has many visitors, moreover. He was once solicited to offer himself as a candidate for a seat in Parliament, but he declined the invitation, preferring this sequestered retreat to the agitation of a Metropolis and the din of debate.

One would be apt to think that, in such a place, and with such habits as those of Mr. Curwen, he must be a happy man. But alas, 'happiness' without alloy is not the lot of man in any station, and we may in vain look for it.

Yachting at the Ferry Inn, approximately 1850.

The viewing station on Claife Heights, Windermere. J. Walton, 1832.

There is one circumstance in Mr. Curwen's case, which must operate as no trifling drawback, upon his apparent happiness, and that is that his eldest son is, and has been from his infancy, deprived of his rational faculty; and what can be a more deplorable calamity than this? – But to return –

We had now arrived at the southern extremity of the island, where we found our old friend the boatman waiting for us. He had, it seems, taken his skiff round the eastern shore. Taking leave of our Island Conductor, we pushed off from this fairy spot; this short trip had been more like a romance than a reality. The sail from the island to the ferry towards which we bent our course, tho' short, was interesting and afforded us an opportunity of seeing from the surface of the lake, the southern or lower extremity of Windermere.

Storrs Hall was on our left hand and the Ferry House on our right. On a woody eminence immediately above the Ferry House the Station arose, amidst rocks and foliage, the dark wooded hill behind it constituting a beautiful relief. By the active exertions of our boatman, we soon reached the

Ferry House jetty, and on our landing, we were once more in our native County of Lancashire.

There is an excellent inn here. Having directed our guide to get some refreshment, we left him with several of his brother craftsmen, and walked directly to the Viewing Station. The road runs for a short distance on the borders of the lake, the margin whereof is planted with tall trees, between which we had varied views of the lake, all of picturesque beauty.

Turning from the lake to our right, by a gradual ascent, we arrived at a romantic Lodge, where the person having the care of the Station resides. The gate was fastened, and we were detained here for some time, owing to the absence of the conductor. We were at length accosted by a female of rather low stature, with brunette face, and pleasing features, with a, "Do you wish to visit the Station, Gentlemen?" and with our replying affirmatively, our fair guide opened the gate and led the way.

After passing the Lodge, the approach to the Station is by a winding ascent. The pathway is elegantly adorned on each side with shrubs, trees and flowers, which with their diversified autumnal hues, has a most romantic effect. Here and there hangs over the walk a huge piece of rock, with twigs and roots fantastically creeping over its surface, and several trees springing from its barren clefts.

Beside the entrance to the Station is a rustic archway, the road thro' which leads to a beautiful shrubbery, wherein is a greenhouse, along the walls of which the woodbine throws its wandering branches. The exterior of the Station presents nothing very outstanding, but as if to render the view from within more striking, the building intercepts the prospect of the surrounding scenery.

We ascended to the Observatory by a short and narrow staircase, and were ushered by our fair guide into an elegantly furnished apartment, three sides of which overlooked the lake. Here we had the east, north and south views of Windermere presented to our notice.

Through the windows of stained glass of different colours, we saw the lake as it appears to the naked eye in the four seasons of the year – the light green giving the vernal tint of spring; the yellow throwing the summer sunbeams upon the foliage; the orange giving the golden cast of autumn and the light blue casting over all the chilly aspect of a winter scene.

Windermere from the viewing station, painting of around 1800.

From this our position, we saw nearly all we had seen during our day's excursion, from the hill, which we had ascended before breakfast, to the lake and the island. We saw these, moreover, as they appear in, spring, summer, autumn and winter. This was a sort of climax to our Windermere views and the effect was magical.

We lingered here for some time as it were, riveted to the spot. I could have taken my Station here for a whole day, but time, the finisher of all things, admonished us to depart. We therefore took leave of this paradisical place, and having remunerated our cicerone, we hastened to the ferry and ordered our aquatic guide to steer us direct to Bowness.

Letter 6

Return to Bowness; front view of Mr. Curwen's house; pleasure boats; departure for Hawkshead; picturesque view from the ferry; disappointment; embarkation; the drover and specimen Westmorland dialect; the ferryman's argument; debarkation; a view of Esthwaite Water; floating islands.

Dear E...,

In our return to Bowness we had a fuller view of Mr. Curwen's house than we had had before, either from the lake or the island, for on our sail from Bowness, the house was on our left, and when we traversed the isle, we had passed at the back of the mansion. The view of the front as we now saw it was very imposing.

The house is of a circular shape and is surmounted by a cupola, which gives it somewhat of an Italian appearance. Fronting the house, and reaching to the verge of the lake is a sloping green lawn edged on both sides with a shrubbery, and variegated with flowers.

The Ferry Inn, Windermere, approximately 1855, from Fenty's collection.

The lake on our return, now presented a more animated scene than it did when we launched from Bowness, for there was now an accession of pleasure-boats upon the water filled with Lakers. In some of the boats we observed elegantly attired females, with their veils flowing in the air, and their red cloaks wrapped around them, to guard their tender frames against the chilly verge of the morning. The smiling features of these fair ones shewed how much they were delighted with the scenery around them.

As our guide had exhausted his budget of information, relative to the different views from the lake, so we, in return for his information, gave him an account of our Lancashire Railroad operations, which greatly delighted and astonished him. Our account of the rapidity of steam carriages, seemed to inspire the old man with a spirit of emulation, for he plied his oars with redoubled dexterity, and he soon brought us to the Bay of Bowness.

Having remunerated our guide who, in answer to inquiring about compensation, told us that his services were to be requited with, "What you please, Gentlemen," and that our host of the White Lion would insert the charge for the boat in the bill, we hurried to the inn, and ordered the gig out forthwith. We soon went through the ceremony of packing up, and settled up with our host, as well as with his throng of satellites, consisting of waiters, boots, chambermaid and hostler, or the 'What-you-please' gentry.

Crack went the whip, and off we started on our journey to Hawkshead, leaving the beautiful village of Bowness, not indeed, without the hope of revisiting it at some future, tho' perhaps distant period.

Northumbrian Engine on new railroad, 1830. W. M. Stuart.

Bowness Bay
Windermere

Wendy M. Stuart.

Some of the smaller isles on Windermere. W. M. Stuart.

The nearest route from Bowness to Hawkshead is over the lake at the ferry, which is half a mile south of the village. This was the road we took, but in our way to the ferry, we lost ourselves, and were obliged to pass through a narrow, steep and uneven lane, to get into the right road. This did not detain us long however, and we soon reached the waterside opposite the Ferry House.

The proprietors of the ferry do not keep boats on the Bowness side of the lake, so whenever a passenger wishes to pass over from that side, he has to 'Halloo' to the boatmen on the opposite shore, which is distant at least half a mile. We hallooed long and loudly without effect, we waved our handkerchiefs, and shouted still more vociferously, and yet no sign of motion on the water.

Having reiterated our shouts, we at length perceived a movement from the wharf by the ferry. It was a very slow movement, however. I was not idle during this period of suspension, for the view from our present position was perhaps one of the most picturesque I had seen, and I took out my pencil and sketched it.

The Ferry House was on the opposite side of the lake, and directly in front of us, the house half embowered in trees; here and there a portion of its white walls visible through the branches; behind the ferry house arose a dark woody hill, with occasional patches of rock, that framed the perspective. A little to the right of the ferry house, a large bay extended itself as far as the foot of the mountain, and still further to the right arose a tuft of trees. To the left of the ferry house, the white turret of the Station was perceptible, and this completed the picture.

When I had about half finished my sketch, the vessel which we had seen move from the ferry house towards us, and which Yates had been watching with much anxiety, suddenly took another direction, and proceeded towards Bowness; it turned out to be a trader. We were now obliged to have recourse again to our signals, and after exerting our vocal powers, and waving our handkerchiefs for somewhere about ten minutes, we perceived a boat with two rowers coming from the ferry house.

This boat's movements were more rapid than the trader's, and were directed towards us, and the large oars moved majestically upon the water. The boat being hauled to the shore, the process of embarkation began. A platform sufficiently broad to admit the widest carriage was placed with one end upon the boat and the other upon the shore. The ferryman then ungirt the horse and led him over the plank, and he (as horses generally are upon the water) was

Loading the ferry with horse and cart, approximately 1870.

perfectly pacific.

The gig was got into the boat in a trice, and we were about to set sail, when a Westmorland drover stept into the boat, who, being an acquaintance of the ferrymen, was, together with his long-nosed sheepdog, allowed his passage gratis. I merely introduce this character to your notice to give you a specimen of the Westmorland dialect, a fine example of which was exhibited in the following short dialogue that took place between the drover and one of the ferrymen.

Boatman, "Heaw han ye gatten rid o yere ware sic sane?"

Drover, "I had but a lile few sheep. And han yea mich wark at t'ferry o leate?"

Boatman, "None sa mitch, but they'll want anither yeand at t'ferry in a bit."

Drover, "Wot, are yea ganging awa?"

Boatman, "Yeah, I'm ganging to Misther Yeakins."

If you pronounce the foregoing as it is written, you may form a pretty good notion of the Westmorland dialect, but as the meaning may puzzle you, I will give it in plain English - it is as follows:

Windermere Lake from Ferry House, 1833.   W. Taylor.

Boatman, "How have you got rid of your cattle so soon?"

Drover, "I had but a few sheep; and have you had much work at the ferry lately?"

Boatman, "Not much, but they will want another hand at the ferry soon."

Drover, "What? Are you about to go away?"

Boatman, "Yes, I am going to Mr. Aikins."

When we had nearly arrived at the other side of the lake, our ears were saluted with a loud holler from behind us. Turning to the place whence the noise proceeded, we perceived a party on the opposite shore waving handkerchiefs, and waiting with a carriage to be ferried over.

Our boatmen, being ordered on their arrival, to do something in the stables instantly, seemed glad to evade this stable performance, by pointing significantly to the carriage party who were now bellowing vociferously, and observed to their master, "Can'na yea see a carriage wearting to be ferried ow'er," and, "Mun'na wea gang fer it?" This interrogation was eventually a conclusive argument, as they returned to the boat, but whether the stable-work was done or not, I cannot say, for it was not, to a certainty, done instanter.

On our debarkation, we were once more in Lancashire, and our horse being quickly attached to the gig, we drove on without stopping at the Ferry House, at which however, there seemed some fashionable company.

After traversing for a short distance the bonny banks of Windermere, we turned off to our right and had soon to surmount a high and precipitous hill, from the top of which a most delightful prospect lay before us. Here we had a view of Esthwaite Water (One of our Lancashire lakes), stretching through a beautiful valley for about the length of two miles, its banks encircled with fine meadows, flowing cornfields and the hills which rose on the further side of the water, shaded with hanging woods.

Here and there was a handsome stone-built mansion to be seen, amongst which Esthwaite Lodge on the opposite shore, and the house of Mr. Galland on the other side, are mainly conspicuous. The western horizon of this extensive view consisted of high hills of which Bowfell and the Langdale Pikes were the most prominent.

The ride from the ferry to Hawkshead was full of interest. On our approach to the latter place, we saw the floating island, an island which floats from one side of the lake to the other. It is but of small dimension and is covered with a few small trees and under-wood. You must understand that this island is not always in motion. When we saw it, it was stationary at the east side of the northern extremity of the lake.

With respect to floating islands, there are some persons who doubt the fact of their existence. I am not such a sceptic, however. There is nothing unnatural in them, nothing incredible in a quantity of earth being disannexed from the shore, and becoming of a texture firm enough, for trees to take root upon. With the mass being unconnected with the soil at the sides and bottom of the lake, it is not unreasonable that it should move about by the wind.

We have the authority of ancient writers for the existence of these islands. Seneca tells of many of them in Italy, and tho' few, if any, are to be met with there now, yet that is no proof of their non-existence formerly. Their motion may have worn them away, which is more than likely.

Pliny also gives an account of a Great Island, which swam about, in the Lake of Cutica, and Pompeius says: "In Lydia there were several islands, so loose in their foundations, that every little accident shook and removed them."

As for the floating islands upon Esthwaite Water, a gentleman, who lives in the neighbourhood, told us that he frequently observed it change its position.

Looking down on Esthwaite Water from the west, 1985.

Letter 7

*Arrival at Hawkshead; a new acquaintance; view from churchyard
and church; the academy; dinner; reasons for not staying at Coniston;
view of Esthwaite Water on the Coniston road; reapers; a lonely lane;
nutting; an alarming incident; Ambleside; a race for lodgings; Low Wood;
Mary, maid of the inn; anger disarmed by beauty.*

Dear E...,

We arrived at Hawkshead about two o'clock, and drove to the Red Lion, a
very good inn, tho' not of very prepossessing exterior. Having ordered dinner, we, to save time, thought it best, whilst the cook was plying at the culi-
nary art, that we should satisfy our curiosity and feast our eyes by looking
thro' the town.

Hawkshead, from a painting on wood, circa 1790.

Having a packet for Mr. Clarke (brother of Mr. Clarke of Preston) we went in the first place to see him. His house is on the outskirts of the town, a neat building with a small garden before it, and is in every way eligible for one who is fond of retirement. We met with a warm welcome from Mr. and Mrs. Clarke and were pressingly invited to partake of some refreshment.

How gratifying it is, when from home, to meet with persons such as these, and how pleasing it is, when in a far country, to fall into the company of those who have some connection with 'Home Sweet Home.' For however capti-vating the objects may be that surround you when abroad, yet there is some-thing more interesting still in meeting accidentally in the course of your trav-els, with one that can converse with you about your own town, and your own acquaintance. Our chitchat with Mr. Clarke naturally turned upon what was going on at Preston; and births, marriages and deaths, trade and improve-ments were the principal topics of our conversation.

After spending some time here, Mr. Clarke offered to show us the town, and to point out the 'Lions' of the place. These however, are neither vast or numerous, for tho' Hawkshead is beautifully situated; yet there is nothing in the town itself to strike the attention. "We don't boast of our town," says our conductor, "but of the scenery about it, and I will take you to a spot from which that scenery may be viewed to most advantage."

We were led to the churchyard, which being on an eminence, commands an extensive prospect of the country for many miles around. The views from hence can scarcely be excelled for beauty and variety by any at the lakes. The eye traverses over a fine fertile valley (through a great part of which flows the lake of Esthwaite Water) and rests upon the distant mountains in the west, amongst which is Coniston Old Man (so called from a huge heap of stones, on its summit, resembling the appearance of an old man). The Langdale Pikes are also prominent.

The immediate vicinity of the town was enlivened by many a Gentlemen's seat, and we were told by our friend at Hawkshead, that there were more independents in the neighbourhood of that town, than in any other county, as a proof of which, he said, that upon an average, there were not less than twelve or fourteen carriages at the church door on a Sabbath day.

The church is a plain, whitewashed edifice and has an antique appearance. It appears, from historical records, to be of the age of the Norman Conquest, and when Furness Abbey was the seat of the Ecclesiastics, Divine Service

The ruins of the monastery.

was performed at this church, by monks belonging to that establishment. The ruins of an old building on the north of the town are shown to the stranger as the remains of the monks' habitation.

It was not the want of curiosity, but the want of time, and perhaps, partially the want of a dinner, that prevented me from visiting this piece of antiquity.

Knowing that Hawkshead was famous for an eminent Classical Academy, I asked our conductor where that academy was, and he pointed to a house near the churchyard, and not many yards from the place where we were then standing.

"Can that," said I, in astonishment, "be the noted Seminary of Hawkshead? That poor dilapidated building, which is more like a parish workhouse than anything I can imagine – can that be the Academy to which scholars have resorted from all parts of the country?"

"Yes," observed my friend, "That is indeed, the place, and I am sorry to add that the Seminary, so noted formerly, has of late, lost much of its importance – it is to be hoped, however," said he, "that by the zealous exertions of Dr. Hickie, the new Master, the school will regain, 'ere long, its former popularity."

After parading the town, we took leave of our new companion, and on our arrival at the Red Lion, we found an excellent dinner provided for us. As our morning trip to the top of the Westmorland Crag had given us a relish for breakfast, so our ride on the banks of a Lancashire Lake had no less whetted our appetite for a Lancashire Dinner.

Both Yates and I made a most hearty repast. We were particularly pleased over it with our waiter, an active little boy of not more than fourteen years old, whose prompt and assiduous attention entitled him to our warm encomium. This may, perhaps, appear to you too trifling a matter to mention, but I assure you that it is a thing of no small moment to a traveller, who wants his dinner and to have his wants readily attended to. We felt the inconvenience of a dilatory waiter, in another part of our tour, as I shall notice hereafter.

You may remember the plan of our route, as settled at Kendal, was to be at Low Wood this evening, and there to remain until the arrival of our friends on the morrow. We had, however, received from Mr. Clarke such a flattering description of Coniston Water, which is only three miles from Hawkshead, that we began to consider whether we had not better alter our plans by going to Coniston that day, and proceed to Low Wood early in the morning.

Upon more mature consideration, however, we resolved to adhere to our original plan, for as we intended, at all events, to reach Keswick the following day, (which is eighteen miles from Low Wood) we should, by going to Coniston, make that day's journey too long, too laborious for the horse, and too rapid for us to see the country as we went along. We determined, accordingly,

The Coniston stage coach outside the Red Lion, approximately 1850.

on the strength of this reasoning, to proceed directly to Low Wood, and to postpone our visit to Coniston Water till some more favourable opportunity.

On leaving Hawkshead we had a journey of six miles before us. It was one of the most delightful evenings that I ever remembered. About half a mile from the town, a most enchanting prospect was spread before us. This view, for richness and variety, was equal to any we had seen on our journey. The whole extent of Esthwaite Lake was perceptible, the nearest point of which was distant about a mile in front of us. The water of this lake, as the 'Historian of Lancashire' observes, seems to glide through the quiet privacy of pleasure grounds, so fine is the turf on its banks, so elegant are its copses, and such an air of peace and retirement reigns over the whole.

Hawkshead Church, 1790.

The town of Hawkshead stood a little on our right, with its church overlooking the vale beneath. At the foot of the hill where the sacred edifice was reared, a white farmhouse was conspicuous, and this contributed to the rusticity of the scene. The foreground of this prospect was enriched with cornfields, and enlivened by groups of reapers gathering in the harvest. We stopped our horse at an elevated point to enable us the better to behold this interesting picture.

Yates's eye (which is ever the quickest-sighted in discovering what is lovely) was fixed steadfastly for some time upon a beautiful female, who stood in the cornfields, regarding the operations of the reapers, and I dare say that if I could, at that moment, have penetrated his thoughts, I should have ascertained that he considered this object in the picture, as the finishing stroke to its perfection.

During our stay here the sun suddenly cast its bright rays upon the lake, which, making it appear like a glassy mirror, produced an effect indescribably magnificent.

Our further progress for two or three miles was through a lane, partly shaded by trees, and partly edged by hills. Though these hills were by no

GROUPS OF REAPERS GATHERING IN THE HARVEST.

means high enough to attract our admiration, yet they were sufficiently so to obstruct our view of the surrounding scenery. There was nothing in this ride remarkable except its loneliness.

We travelled for some time without seeing so much as a cot on the roadside or meeting with a passenger in the way. The road being very uneven, our progress was rather slow, indeed in some places, owing to the steepness of the ascent, we were obliged to dismount from our vehicle and trudge on foot.

This lonely lane, however, was not entirely devoid of its attractions to my companion, for as he was fond of 'nutting,' he had here full scope to occupy himself in that way. Every now and then I saw him amongst the branches of a hazel tree, and anon, he presented me with the fruits of his labour. I, not being so nimble in the climbing of trees, was occupied in gathering blackberries and wild raspberries, which were plentifully scattered in my path. We had thus ample means of helping ourselves to a cheap repast.

How unlike this are the lanes in the neighbourhood of a populous town where the urchins strip every bough, leaving scarcely a blackberry, or a nut or raspberry to ripen. We thus sauntered in this lovely lane for a mile or so without meeting anyone; and Yates had strolled a considerable way before me, when an incident occurred which gave me momentary uneasiness.

Just on turning an angle of the lane, a suspicious looking man suddenly made his appearance. He was strong built and tall, too well dressed, I thought, for a beggar, and yet too uneasily clad for a tourist of Pleasure. He had not the honest look of a Rustic, but had a countenance of a rather questionable character.

The man came up to me, and I thought was about to accost me. I was alarmed, and the more so as my companion was considerably before me. When this man got up to me, he craved my charity; I was glad that was all he wanted, but more glad when I saw him behind me. It was rather strange that this mendicant passed my companion without speaking a word to him.

After this occurrence we mounted our vehicle and rode at a brisk pace until we got to the end of this solitary lane, which brought us to the head, or northern extremity of our favourite lake of Windermere, the view of which opened suddenly before us.

We were now near Ambleside and drove past several handsome houses, one of which in particular, from its antique appearance, caught our eye, and which we learned belonged to Mr. Brancker, the present Mayor of Liverpool. These houses are delightfully situated on sloping grounds, and command extensive views of the lake of Windermere.

As there was no necessity for passing thro' Ambleside on our way to Low Wood, we did not do so, but turned off a little in the west and round the head

The head of Lake Windermere, 1870.

W.M.STUART. WE DID ALL WE COULD TO OVERTAKE THE
CURRICLE IN ORDER TO SECURE A PRIORITY OF BEDS, BUT
WITH ALL OUR EFFORTS, IT ARRIVED AT THE INN BEFORE US,

of the lake. The road to Low Wood was very interesting, and was, perhaps, rendered more so to us by the contrast which it presented to the lonely lane through which we had just travelled.

We met and overtook many tourists here, more indeed, than we had seen at any place on our route. This was probably owing to our being nearer to Ambleside, which is generally made a central point, or nightly position of Lakers. I call it a central or nightly position, because here tourists take up their station for some time, driving in all directions during the day and return-ing hither to take up their quarters for the night.

Passing along the eastern banks of the lake, there arose between us, and the water, the lofty branches of the fir, and poplar, with the spreading foliage of the larch and ash. The road is here and there overshadowed by trees, which form a pleasant avenue or shady grove. Through the foliage, a view of the lake occasionally breaks in upon one's sight, and with its sloping banks of ver-nal green, constitutes a delightful picture. To heighten the whole, the setting sun was now shedding his ruby rays around, which was a warning to the tourist to repair to his evening quarters.

We were not far from the Inn at Low Wood (for there is but one inn there) when a curricle passed us with a lady and gentleman in it, and as we were fear-ful, from the groups of Lakers we had seen on the way, that the inn might be full of visitors, we did all we could to overtake the curricle in order to secure a priority of beds, but with all our efforts, it arrived at the inn before us.

It happened luckily however, that we could be accommodated with beds, and we therefore alighted, and were ushered into a front apartment, which overlooked the Lake. Low Wood Inn is pleasantly situated on the banks of Windermere, is about a mile and a half from Ambleside and five miles from Bowness.

It is an inn much frequented by visitors, there being many delightful views in the neighbourhood. The greater propinquity of the mountains renders the scenery about Low Wood more magnificent than that about Bowness. Coniston Old Man lifts his stupendous head, and Scafell and the Langdale Pikes form the extreme background.

The lake here swells out in a fine open bay, and several pretty white villas grace the shores. The inn is not more than 30 yards from the margin of the water and three tall poplar trees rising majestically in front of the house, at a distance of about ten yards from the lake, add to the picturesque beauty of the place.

Having taken possession of our chambers and arranged our toilets for the night, we spent some time at the bow window of our sitting room admiring the scenery I have just been attempting to describe. Several boats passed in review before us, taking company to their evening destination; some bound for Ambleside, some for Bowness and some for Low Wood. One of these

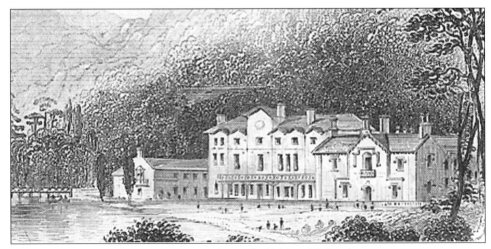

The Low Wood Hotel, 1825.   W. Banks.

boats attracted the particular attention of my fellow tourist, being rowed by two elegantly dressed females.

The evening clouds now began to creep along the sides, and rest upon the summits of the distant mountains, and in a little time, the objects without becoming indistinguishable, we began to look for sources of amusement within; so drawing near the fire, our first consideration was to order tea.

We rang the bell, but our call was unattended. We now knew how to appreciate the value of an active waiter, by knowing the want of one. Such a one as the Hawkshead youth would

Yates in 1830, drawn by Isaac Simpson.

have been a great improvement in the accommodation at Low Wood – the bell was rung again and again, with still no answer to the summons.

We were losing all stock of patience that we possessed, and Yates began to vow what he would do when anyone appeared – he would, "Blow them up, Aye, that he would!"

Now, I am an advocate for peace; at all times I hate chiding, and would rather put up with a trifling inconvenience (as I conceived this to be), than to set fire to the train of my angry feelings, and 'blow up' the person who is the cause of my displeasure.

I ventured to interpose with my principal of forbearance in the way of my friend's ire; but the more I endeavoured to dissuade him from giving vent to his feelings, the more determined he seemed upon an explosion.

At length the maid of the inn appeared, and Mary, (for that was her name) possessed indeed a handsome figure and a prepossessing countenance; and with a smile of true Westmorland simplicity, she asked our commands. I anxiously waited the issue.

"Little," thought I, "does Mary know what fiery indignation is about to be poured upon her head – now for it!"

But mark the consequence. What I had been unable to accomplish by argument, Mary had, in a moment, effected by her winning looks, and instead of my companion pouring forth a tirade of angry words, he selected from his vocabulary the most soft and loving expressions he could well make choice of.

As soon as Mary's back was turned, I burst out into a loud fit of laughter, at the victory that she had gained over my fellow traveller.

"This is an admirable mode of chide," said I. "This is a mild species of remonstrance – well, well, my friend, I find where reason cannot prevail with you, beauty can, and Mary's smiles have been far more potent than my arguments." Whenever Yates tells me of the Burton Beauty I can easily retaliate by joking to him about his gentle chiding of Mary, the maid of the inn.

My companion's remonstrance had not much effect in quickening Mary's future movements, but he seemed satisfied, after his first frustration, to let her take her own time in preparing the tea. Procrastination did not matter much, for we had not any wherewith to occupy our time, save in conversation, which was as easily carried on before our tea, as after. In Mary's time, the whistling urn and smoking toast were set before us, and if the maid was dilatory in her vocation, we were no less so in performing our parts.

We had scarcely finished tea, when a stranger was introduced to the room, who had just arrived in a gig. He was a young man, and from his luggage he appeared to be a commercial traveller. He had not, however, the vivacity or loquacity generally belonging to that class of men; but tho' he was not a man of many words, he was far from being like the mute old gentleman, or the two insulated Cantabs that we met with at Bowness.

He travelled a little about the Lakes, upon which our conversation turned. He told us of what he had seen, and in return we gave him a narrative of our excursions – of our trip to the mountain crag at Bowness, the sail upon Windermere, the island, the station, the ferry, the lake of Esthwaite Water, the town of Hawkshead, the solitary route between that place and Ambleside, and lastly, Yates could not refrain from telling (to my great surprise) of the tediousness of the waiters at the Low Wood Inn.

Our new companion retired to rest before us, and we spent the remains of

The Low Wood Inn on Windermere, 1825.   G. Pickering.

the evening in chatting about our friends at home. I retired to rest at last, well pleased with the events of the day, and was then soon overcome by nature's sweet restorer, balmy sleep.

> *While o'er my limbs, sleep's soft dominion spread,*
> *Upon my soul, fantastic measures tread –*
> *On fairy Isles – or sailed along the shore,*
> *Or walked the Grove, or climbed the Craggy Tor.*

Letter 8

*Morning walk at Low Wood; views from the eminence behind the inn;
a view of Windermere; head from the banks of the lake; a game of bowls;
a southerner and two Yorkshiremen at breakfast; nuisance at the inn;
our departure from Low Wood; Ambleside; Rydal; an ancient guide.*

Dear E...,

My repose was somewhat prematurely disturbed by the barking of dogs without, which, I supposed, were aroused by the timely movements of the servants about the inn. The sound reverberated from hill to hill, with Sonorousness truly astonishing.

I got up soon after sunrise, and being anxious to ascertain the state of the weather, I looked out of my chamber window, which was directly opposite the lake. There was haziness over the water, and the tops of the distant mountains

Head of Windermere, 1835. G. Pickering.

were covered with clouds. These signs indicated a dubious day; it was fair, however, and having awoken my companion, we strolled out soon after seven o'clock.

As we had the morning before experienced much pleasure and advantage in a mountain trip, so we were induced to adopt the same plan on this occasion, and accordingly, directed our footsteps to the most elevated position that we could perceive in the neighbourhood of Low Wood.

This was a field behind the inn, which was not so near as high as the crag at Bowness, but it was high enough to afford a commanding view of the country around us. Having reached the top of the field, I sate upon a stone, and whilst my friend was rummaging amongst the branches of his favourite hazel trees, I sketched a sort of bird's-eye view of the picture beneath and before me.

There was nothing particularly striking in this view, beyond what we had seen from Bowness Crag, except in the greater variety of distant mountain scenery. We were somewhat nearer the Coniston and Langdale hills.

The prospect was varied and interesting; the corn-ricks formed a pretty foreground, the top of the inn was just perceptible over a rising ground, and the three tall poplars in front of the hotel added to the beauty of the scene. The white cottages on the opposite side of the lake afforded a fine relief to the hills behind them, and several handsome and romantic villas upon rising grounds, on our right hand side, served as a finishing stroke to this pretty picture.

After spending about half an hour here, we proceeded to the banks of the lake, whence we had a magnificent view of the scenery at Windermere Head. On our right, a fine row of trees skirted the margin of the water. Above these was seen a handsome stone-built mansion of a curious, conical form, with a bright green sloping lawn in front of it, which finely contrasted with the dark green of the trees immediately beyond, and the azure of the distant hills further in the background.

We had hence too, a fine view of the front of the inn and of the trees before the door. The bowling green formed a pleasing feature in this picture, with its long shed reaching from one end of the green to the other. The lake here swells out into an extensive bay, and there stood a rustic boathouse not far from us. The high hills of Rydal Head and Helvellyn were seen in the distance, and the whole formed a scene, not inferior to any we had before witnessed.

Lakers at the head of the lake.   W. M. Stuart.

I have already had occasion to notice my companion's fondness for a game of bowls, and the sight of the bowling green instinctively, as it were, drew his footsteps thitherwards. Indeed, I believe the finest scenery in the universe, could not induce him to forgo his favourite amusement, when a fitting opportunity offers, for trundling the bowl. I was no match for him at this game, but there was no better match at hand, and so he must needs invite me, and notwithstanding my protestations of inability to cope with him, he was really so pressing, that to please him I complied with his request. After spending half an hour at this diversion (at which I need hardly say that my companion was triumphantly victorious), and finding that the exercise had given a tone to our appetites, we adjourned to the inn.

Here we found three gentlemen at breakfast. One of them, we afterwards learned, (for travellers have a licence you know, to be inquisitive) was from the south of England, and the other two were Yorkshiremen. In the first moment, I recognised the gentleman who passed us in the curricle the evening before, on our road to Low Wood.

He was, apparently, about the age of forty, of genteel demeanour, he was affable, but his conversation was of that sort, which had in it a good deal of self importance and superiority over those whom he thought knew less of the world than himself. He talked largely of his travels; and the two more unassuming, less talkative, tho' perhaps not less intelligent Yorkshiremen, speaking in praise of these lakes, which far surpassed any scenery they had beheld before, the more grandiloquent southerner burst forth into a highly coloured narrative of *his* travels, comparing, as he went along with his story, the different lakes that *he* had seen.

"After visiting the sublime scenery of Wales," said the traveller, " I was recommended to visit these lakes of Westmorland and Cumberland, which I confess, have much of the sublime and beautiful joined together."

"I suppose I shall now be told that the lakes of Scotland are still more superior in both respects. I may be prevailed upon, by the admirers of Caledonia, to visit *them*."

" When I have seen the lakes of Scotland, I may be informed, by those who are fond of foreign parts, that all I have seen in England, Wales and Scotland cannot be compared with the lakes of Italy."

The Yorkshiremen, whose travels, I dare say, had not been far beyond their native country, listened to this account with considerable attention. We found from the subsequent conversation of this trio, that they had met before at some other place in their tour, for they were speaking of certain individuals that they had encountered in their journey, and it was asked by one, what had become of the young gentleman in the light smoking jacket, and his companion? This question was immediately succeeded by a smile on the countenance of the whole party, and from certain observations which fell, I immediately recognised as the subject of conversation, the two Coxcomb Cantabs,

"... A great number of dogs at Low Wood."

whom we had met at Bowness and who, it was evident, had stood no higher in the estimation of the Yorkshiremen than in ours!

We tarried at the Low Wood for about an hour after breakfast, rambling about the fields, through the lanes and on the bank of the lake. There is one thing that cannot escape the observation of the visitors of Low Wood Inn, and that is the great number of dogs there. I verily believe that there were more of these animals at this inn than we saw in the whole course of our northern tour. Here were dogs of all kinds and sizes; from the rough haired sheepdogs to the curly haired lapdog of a lady – I very much doubt whether His Majesty reaps his due from all these animals. They are annoyingly numerous, and so thought the pretty maid Mary who, "Could na tell why ma Maister kept sa many, but they are very troublesome."

It was now past ten o'clock, and as we had expected the arrival of our Kendal friends at an earlier hour than that, we began to doubt whether they would come at all. As we had seen all that was worth seeing at Low Wood, our further remaining there we considered lost time, and our time was precious. We concluded, therefore, to proceed onward, and to leave word with our host at the Low Wood Inn to inform our companions, should they arrive soon, that we would wait for them at Ambleside.

Having ordered our gig out, paid our reckoning, and taken leave of our friends at Low Wood (not forgetting Mary), we were once more on our way to Ambleside, passing the toll house at the head of the lake, at Waterside, and proffered our dues there.

The toll gate at Waterhead.

I have already described to you the scenery on this road, and the distance to Ambleside being but a mile and a half, we determined upon going direct to Rydal, which is a mile further, visit the waterfall at that place, and then return to Ambleside, to wait the arrival of our companions.

We consequently passed thro' the town without

Langdale Pikes near Rydal.   W. M. Stuart.

stopping. On leaving Ambleside we had to descend a steep hill, and afterwards, the road to Rydal presented some enchanted views. Several handsome villas were scattered on our right and left as we rode along the valley;
and just before we reached Rydal Hall (the seat of Lady Fleming), there was,
I think, one of the prettiest landscapes I ever saw.

A rustic bridge stretches over a rivulet; several romantic cottages stand on
the hither side. Over the bridge the head of Rydal Water is visible. The lake
winds to the right, and is skirted on the further side by mountains, some of
which are covered with wood, and others with barren heath. On our approach
to the rustic bridge of which I have just now spoken, we overtook an honest
looking Westmorland rustic, whom we requested to direct us, how to proceed
to get a view of the Cascades.

"Gang a wee bit fur'," said he, "and ye'al come to a turn o' the leane to
yeare reet yeand; and theire ye'll finnd some boddy wha'ill gan wi ye to't
hoose o' the guide."

Rydal Hall, 1980. W. M. Stuart.

You must know that the Rydal Waterfalls are in the demesnes of Lady Fleming who, out of kindness, has given to an old woman in the neighbourhood a privilege, alternately with one of her Ladyship's own servants, of shewing the Cascades to strangers, and consequently of raising a little money by that means.

In obedience to the directions of the rustic (as far as we could understand them), we directed our course onward, till we got to the turn to our right hand, where we soon ascertained where the old guide to the waterfalls dwelt. It happened to be her turn to shew the falls, and she shortly introduced herself to our notice

The old woman had seen more than the average number of years allotted to human existence, having arrived at the good old age of *four* score years and ten. Notwithstanding her great age, she was frank, nimble and talkative, and in the comprehensive phrase of the country, she was what was termed, 'A canny old blade.'

We left the gig at the old dame's cottage, where she assured us, that, "They were all honest folk in Westmorland," and calling out to one of her grandchildren, "Johnny, Johnny, keep an e'e to't gig!" she proceeded up the hill, and we followed.

Letter 9

Rydal Waterfalls; ascent to the upper and descent to the lower fall;
sudden introduction to the latter; beauty in miniature; a partial judge

Dear E...,

Our aged guide mounted the hill with astonishing rapidity. On our right hand lay the demesnes of Lady Fleming, separated from us by a stone wall. We passed on our left the neat chapel of Rydal, a little behind which stands the romantic seat of the poet Wordsworth.

Having nearly reached the top of the hill, our cicerone unlocked the wicker gate, and introduced us to the plantation belonging to Rydal Hall. Here we

Rydal Mount, the seat of Wordsworth.   Fenty's collection.

first heard the murmuring of the distant waterfall, which fell upon our ears like the sound of the sea waves, or the noise of a tumultuous assembly, when heard at a distance.

Our conductor led us for a considerable distance through the grounds by an irregular beaten track. Having passed behind the hall, we came at length to a narrow glen, thro' which a meandering streamlet flowed. We then began to ascend a winding, woody walk, passing at times along the brink of the streamlet. The water, owing to its steep descent, ran rapidly down the rivulet, and though the stream had many obstacles to encounter in its way, yet it overcame them by leaping over or winding round the rocks or branches. It seemed as if the main object of the stream was to reach as soon as possible the bosom of Windermere, where, after a troublesome journey, it reposed in perfect quietude.

The roaring of the cataract fell more distinctly on our ears as we advanced up the hill, and we expected the cascade to burst upon our sight every moment. Shortly afterwards, Yates, who was a little in advance, called out, "There! There it is!" And there it was indeed, roaring and foaming, and gushing from rock to rock with an impetuosity truly amazing, and scattering the foam of its turbulent waters all around. Although we were at many yards distance, the spray fell upon us like drizzling rain.

The pool formed by the cascade was clear as crystal, and its dark green colour finely contrasted with the white foam created by the gushing of the waters. The high rocks on each side of the cataract were rendered as smooth as glass by the continual clashing of the water against their sides, and where the water did not touch them, the moss and the ivy occupied the space. Several tall trees shot their high heads from each side above the highest rocks; other trees scattered their branches across the agitated stream, and created an embowering shade.

It was under such shade that we took our station, and there, about midway up the fall, we stood gazing in astonishment at the wonder of creation, struck with admiration at the grandeur of the scene, which was novel to both of us.

Here we remained for some time, and would probably have remained much longer, had not our ancient cicerone beckoned to us to follow her, intimating at the same time that she had something more to shew us.

She led us by the same winding path by which we had arrived at the fall, down the hill, thro' the glen, by the rivulet and out at the wicket, by which we had at first entered the grounds of Lady Fleming. We were then conducted

through another gateway a little
lower down the hill, and were now
in the principal avenue, which
runs in front of the hall.

We thence had a pretty good
view of the mansion. It is beautifully situated upon a rising
ground, and is surrounded by fine
woods. The high hill of Nabs
Wood is seen at the rear of the
hall, and Gate Crag rises in the
distance in front of it.

We traversed a beautifully
winding walk, gradually with-
drawing from the hall, till we came
to the summit of a sloping bank,
which overlooks the valley. This
vale was thickly strewn with trees,
so that we could not see the murmuring stream, which ran along it.

Advancing a little further down
the hill, we heard a noise as if

The upper falls. H. Gastineau.

from the gushing of waters, and we concluded that we could not be far from
another cataract. Near the place where we stood, there was an old, and apparently weather-beaten summer or garden house, but as this had nothing very
captivating in its exterior appearance, it did not claim much of our attention.
Our eyes were more directed to the romantic valley beneath us, and our ears
to the sound of the disturbed waters.

Our guide advanced towards the summerhouse, however, and requested us
to follow her. We did so. She suddenly opened the door, and a scene presented itself to our notice, an adequate description of which I cannot pretend to
give you. I must content myself with observing that through an opening on
the other side of the summerhouse, we saw immediately before us, and at a
distance of not more than a dozen yards, a beautiful miniature cascade falling
from an elevation of, I should think, about eighteen feet.

On each side arose perpendicular rocks, which, like those at the upper fall,

The lower falls. G. Pickering.

were partially covered with moss, and in some places, as smooth as glass by the continual washing of the water. Some fine tall pine trees overtopped the highest cliff, whilst trees of lesser size, and of a more rambling nature, spread their branches from one side of the stream to the other.

Across the chasm, a rustic bridge was thrown; this bridge led to a cottage, the white walls of which were visible through the foliage, and the smoke from the chimney curling upward towards heaven, was not without its effect. The water, which came tumbling from rock to rock, washed the walls of the summerhouse in which we stood.

The whole space which this interesting scene occupied was very limited, but contracted tho' space was, it comprehended more of the picturesque than I should have conceived it possible to comprise, within so small a compass. Speaking of this scene, the editor of *Gray's Letters* observed that:

"Nature has here performed everything in little, that she usually executes in her larger scale, and on that account, like the miniature painter, seems to have finished every part of it in a studied manner.

"Not a little fragment of a rock thrown into the basin, not a single stem of brushwood that starts from the craggy sides, but has a picturesque meaning, and the little central current, dashing down a cleft of the darkest coloured stone, produces an effect of light and shadow, beautiful beyond description. This little theatrical scene might be painted as large as the original, on a canvas not bigger than those usually dropt in the opera house."

My companion and I were so taken by surprise at the sudden introduction to such a scene, that we simultaneously exclaimed, "Astonishing!"

"Beautiful!" "Admirable!" "This surpasses all we have hitherto seen!"

The old dame's ears caught our laudatory epithets, and she evinced no trifling degree of delight at our commendatory ejaculations, which evidently led her into a train of thought that she loved to indulge in.

She began to decant upon the superior beauty of the cascades at Rydal, over those of her neighbours at Ambleside. As we had not seen the latter, we could not tell to which the palm belonged, but we were much amused by the old woman's energetic tone in speaking the praises of her own.

I could not help suspecting that there might be a little prejudice mixed up with our cicerone's judgement, nor is that to be wondered at, for a prejudice in favour of one's own is universal. Every mother thinks her own child the loveliest, the inhabitants at the poles fancy that nothing can equal the beauty of their ice clad regions, whilst the dwellers of the southern climes wonder how anyone can be so stupid as to not admire the scenes of their country above that of any other.

But to come nearer the point, the people of Westmorland think that their scenery far surpasses that of their Cumbrian neighbours. The latter, on the other hand, conceive that theirs cannot be equalled.

Just so, the old guide at Rydal would have it that her waterfalls (for that is what she called them) were far superior to Stockgill Force at Ambleside. It was no little cause for the old woman's boasting that a party of Lakers, a few days before, had told her that altho' her waterfalls were not so large as that of Stockgill Force, yet they were far more beautiful and picturesque.

Whatever opinion I might have formed of the comparative excellence of the rival waterfalls after seeing them both, I know not, but this I can say, is that it would be difficult to find in the whole range of lake scenery, as much of picturesque beauty within the same compass as is to be seen from the summerhouse of Lady Fleming.

I made an attempt to sketch the scene, but the passing thought of our Kendal companions, and of the possibility of their having arrived at Ambleside, induced me to leave the sketch unfinished. We hastened to our gig, and having recompensed our cicerone liberally, as we thought, (but who, by the bye, did not seem very grateful for the boon) and for her grandson, Johnny for his guardian, "E'e", we returned to Ambleside, highly gratified with our trip to Rydal.

Letter 10

Ambleside; arrival of our Kendal friends; dinner at the Commercial Inn; departure; our cavalcade; the decorum of Westmorland rustics; Rydal Lake; an incident with a country dame; Vale of Grasmere; comparison of the lakes; the Swan Inn at Grasmere.

Dear E...,

We drove to the Commercial Inn, which has a very genteel exterior, but we soon found that the accommodations here were not such as we expected from the outward appearance of the house. Our first inquiry was whether there were any arrivals from Kendal; the answer to such inquiry being in the negative, we began to despair of seeing our friends at all. That event was still possible, however, and as you may remember, we had had some experience in our tour of the uncertainty of keeping an appointment with punctuality,

Ambleside, 1830.   W. M. Stuart.

86

when one has the chances or mis-chances of travelling, to encounter. So on the present occasion, we thought it best to calculate upon such mischances, and to wait a few hours at Ambleside for the arrival of our companions.

Ambleside is an ancient market town, and you will be able to form an idea of its size when I tell you that it contains about a thousand inhabitants. This may be called the metropolis of the Westmorland lakes, as Keswick is of the Cumbrian waters, and as Ambleside possesses a central situation, it is much resorted to; here the tourist makes his headquarters and the centre of his movements.

Entering Ambleside.

In our rambles about the town, seeing what we could see, and picking up what information we could procure from the rustics whom we met, (which was a favourite occupation with me, tho' it called forth occasionally the censure of my companion) we strolled down a lane, which apparently led past the foot of a lofty mountain.

I was contemplating an ascent of this hill, and was interrogating a country girl as to its name, height, the way to the top, and the probable time it would take to attain the summit, when my brother tourist, who was at some distance from me, put a sudden stop to my rising notions by calling out, "They are coming, they are coming!"

Turning my attention to the point to which my friend directed it, I saw a horseman preceding a gig, coming up the lane at a rapid rate. As they came nearer, we recognised Hamilton, Medcalfe and Crosthwaite; we hailed them with a loud shout, and Yates ran to tell them to drive to the Commercial Inn.

By the time I reached the inn, our companions had alighted, and Medcalfe and Crosthwaite were regretting that we had not taken up our quarters at the

Bridge House, Ambleside, 1834. T. Allom.

Salutation. "A much better inn," said they, "than the Commercial."

The first congratulations being over, we ordered dinner from the waiter, for one and all had purchased a most hearty appetite by our morning's ride.

Anticipating a sumptuous repast at such a goodly looking inn as this, what was our astonishment at the reappearance of the waiter, with the singular interrogation of, "Gentlemen, would you prefer a lamb chop, or a mutton chop for dinner?"

On the question being put, our Westmorland friends stared at each other as much as to say, "This question is a slander upon our own county, and what will our Lancashire friends think of us?"

At length, Crosthwaite broke the silence, which had pervaded for a minute or two, by asking the waiter what he meant by, "A lamb chop for *five* of us?"

"Really, Mr. Waiter" said he, "What are you dreaming about? Have you not such a thing as a joint of meat in the house? Nay, if there be one in the town let us have it, by all means!" With these commands issued, the waiter disappeared, and soon afterwards returned, with the far more rational announcement, that a joint of meat was being prepared for us.

Over dinner, we narrated the events of our journey since we parted from our friends. Hamilton told us of his trip to Carlisle, whilst Medcalfe and Crosthwaite entertained us with a humorous account of their journey back from Bowness to Kendal on Monday evening.

Soon after dinner we left Ambleside – it was a beautiful afternoon.

Crosthwaite rode his mettlesome mare and acted as our outrider. Hamilton and Medcalfe followed immediately after in their gig; then Yates and I brought up the rear. If such a cavalcade had been progressing in the neighbourhood of Preston, it would have been an object of gazing to the country people; but it was not so in the country through which we were travelling.

It is a circumstance not unworthy of remark, that in travelling round the lakes, there is not seen amongst the rustics, in even the most retired places, that unpleasant surveillance, or vulgar stare, or impertinent shout, which you are used to be annoyed with, in the neighbourhood of a populous town. I cannot account for this, but such is the fact, and it redounds to the credit of the country people.

Our road for a mile and a half after quitting Ambleside was what Yates and I had traversed on our pleasant trip to the Rydal Waterfalls. I now regretted that when we were there, we did not walk as far as Rydal Mount, the residence of Wordsworth. Time

Wordsworth. W. M. Stuart.

would not permit us to redress the omission now.

A short ride beyond Rydal Hall brought us suddenly in sight of Rydal Water, one of the smallest, but at the same time, one of the most picturesque of the lakes. It runs silently along a quiet and secluded wooded vale, and is lined by lofty hills, of which Loughrigg Fell is on the one side, and Rydal Head on the other. These hills gradually ascend from the very verge of the water, some more, and others less, abruptly. The lake contains several islets, which are beautifully reflected in the water. Here and there on the banks is seen an ivy covered, or whited cottage, peeping thro' a rich and variegated foliage.

This is such a scene that the admirers of Zimmerman would select for a retreat. The profound tranquillity of the lake, and the dark, deep shade of the woods and mountains, combine to create such a scene, as the most

Rydal Water.   Fenty's collection.

enthusiastic admirers of that author of 'Solitude' cannot fail to love.

The prospect before us was beginning to touch the melancholy chord of my heart, when the feeling was suddenly checked by the following trifling incident. A trio of female rustics, with sickles in their hands, at this moment passed us. From their appearance, they might be a mother and her two daughters. As the mother passed Yates and me (our companions being somewhat in advance), she said to the younger one, but loud enough for us to hear, "I've seen mony a gentleman travel this way, but Ah nivver saw sie a parcel o' Gawks afore!"

Being ignorant of the cause of such a remark that was so uncomplimentary to our companions, we called out to ascertain what was the cause of the dame's displeasure. We found that Crosthwaite had asked the young damsels if they wanted husbands; a harmless question, it is true, but perhaps the mother thought it was an insult to modesty, and I do not blame her for resenting it.

When any new and striking object was about to present itself to our notice, Crosthwaite, who was well acquainted with the country, and who still acted as our advance guard, intimated the same to Medcalfe and Hamilton, and they in turn to us, at first by outstretched hand or uplifted hand, and afterwards by oral communication. It was one of these signals that now apprised us of our approach to Grasmere.

The various pictures I had seen of Grasmere led me to form a romantic notion of it, and if the lover of the fair sex attaches a romantic idea to the name of Buttermere, so the lover of rural scenery attaches an idea not less romantic to the vale of Grasmere. Its very name is 'rural.'

The valley now opened upon us, in the bosom of which the lake stretches for about a mile in length. This lake is somewhat broader than that of Rydal, and the surrounding hills form a more extensive amphitheatre. The cottages too, being more numerous, and the meadows more abundant, renders the prospect here, one of lively contrast, to that of the silent and solitary Vale of Rydal.

The lakes of Rydal and Grasmere can be likened to two infant sisters, the one of a grave and melancholy cast, and the other of a lively and cheerful character. What rendered the latter lake still more lively was the sun, which was verging towards a western cloudless sky, and cast his ruddy rays upon the expanse of water as we approached it; he also, at that moment, gilded the

Grasmere, 1831. Isaac Simpson.

village windows, and caught the steeple of the little church, which was now seen immediately before us.

One of the most prominent objects in this view was the hill called Helm Crag, of a conical shape, rising at the head of the village. At the top of this hill are some broken fragments of rock, which are said to bear the resemblance of an old woman in a cowering posture, or the likeness of a lion and a lamb, in the act of fulfilling that scriptural prophesy of universal peace, when, "These animals shall lie down together."

The latter similitude is, in my opinion, the more striking of the two, but these resemblances are more distinguishable just after you leave the village, on the way to Thirlmere. Indeed, we could not easily perceive the likeness, as we approached Grasmere from Rydal.

You must be aware that in travelling rapidly through the country, I can only give you a general picture of the scenery. Many beauties escape the eye of the equestrian, and as experience is far the best schoolmistress, I would recommend that whenever you take a tour of the lakes, you traverse as much of the country on foot as possible. The day being far advanced, and as we were desirous of reaching Keswick that night, we were obliged to travel at a more rapid rate than we were wont, and the consequence was, that we lost much of the beautiful scenery that surrounded us.

The mode, in which we travelled therefore, must be my apology for giving you so short a description of the beautiful vale of Rydal and Grasmere. We drove rapidly past the neat white church of Grasmere to the Swan Inn, the most romantic inn you ever saw, and there we alighted in order to give our horses some refreshment, as well as to take a little ourselves.

The Swan Inn, 1995.

We made but a short stay here, but quite long enough to convince us that the host of the Swan understood well the 'Art of Overcharging,' or may I say, 'Imposing upon Strangers.' For to our great astonishment, when our bill was presented, we found that we were charged five and twenty per cent more than we had been charged for the same beverage at any place on our journey.

I suppose they charge here on the principal that they are not likely to see the same customer again, and the host may depend upon it, for he does not act in a way to secure a second visit to his house. We remonstrated at the glaring imposition, but in vain; we called for the hostess, but she was not to be seen.

We had one mode of making up for the overcharge, however, and we determined to avail ourselves of it. This was to give the 'What-you-please' gentry of the Establishment, what we did please, and that was nothing at all – to pay the bill and nothing but the bill! Then, driving at a quick pace, we left the hostler and waiter grumbling behind us, but, as a sort of consolation, we told them we should remember them the next time we visited Grasmere, and I think in this, we shall keep our promise.

Letter 11

Different distribution of our party; rugged rocks; Dunmail Raise; various traditions of it; our arrival in Cumberland; gloomy lake of Thirlmere; approach of evening; cimmerian darkness; dangerous driving; council of safety; the smithy of St. John's Vale.

Dear E...,

On leaving Grasmere, our party was distributed in a different manner, from the position in which it had hitherto maintained. Medcalfe and I rode together in his gig, and Crosthwaite and Hamilton in ours. As for Yates, he foolishly resolved to ride the mettled mare of Crosthwaite. He, however, very soon found (but not until after a narrow escape from a somerset), that the safer way

Dunmail Raise, 1830. J. Harwood.

94

was to betake himself to his gig, and he surrendered the mare to its master, who knew better how to manage it.

The distance from Grasmere to Keswick is eleven miles. The road is very mountainous; on one side you have stupendous hills, and on the other in many places, steep precipices. Here and there the road is so narrow and so unguarded from chasms at the side, as to render it unsafe for carriages to pass, even in the daytime. It was no pleasant idea, therefore, to be benighted on such a road as this, and consequently, our main object was to get over as much ground in as little time as possible.

Having proceeded about two miles from Grasmere, we were passing through a deep and dark valley, when our friend Crosthwaite called out, that we were just approaching Dunmaile Raise.

The name was no sooner mentioned, than it awoke a train of antiquarian ideas within me. Dunmaile Raise is a heap of paving stones. These separate the counties of Westmorland and Cumberland, and if the guidebooks speak truth, these stones have been where they are now, ever since the Heptarchy, or for a period of nine hundred years.

Some writers say that the Raise originally marked the boundaries of England and Scotland, as they now do the limits of two counties. Others say that the stones are monumental of a sanguinary battle, fought on the spot between Edward I and Dunmaile, the Last King of Cumberland; in which battle Dunmaile was defeated, and afterwards, with his two sons, put to death. His kingdom of Cumberland was given to Malcolm, King of Scotland.

The superstitious, too, assign their reasons for this huge heap of stones. The tradition with them is that during a race with the Giants (and you know from the history of Jack the Giant Killer, that Cumberland was their favourite dwelling place), a Giant stood with one foot upon this mountain, and the other upon that, and having his apron full of pebbles, he cast them into the vale below, where they still remain.

This last story is as rational as that of the man who is said to have lately stood with one foot upon St. Paul's and the other upon Westminster Abbey, whilst he drank up the Thames.

Be the origin of the stones what it may, there is little doubt that they have been there for many centuries, which circumstance alone, renders them an object of interest to the antiquarian, and this interest is not a little increased by the first two mentioned traditional recounts of their accumulation.

The place where the stones are seen is a lonely stretch, and it still seemed more so to us through the dim twilight by which we beheld it, and the solemn darkness of the surrounding mountains, added to the solemnity.

This spot is a favourite retreat for gypsies, and travellers frequently see those outlandish vagrants, at a distance from the roadside, seated round a few burning embers, with their pot suspended between two cross sticks. I doubt not, that many a time has the spoil of the Cumberland farmers' hen roost, been here doled out among these hungry itinerants.

The Cherry Tree tavern, 1860.

Having passed the Raise, we were now in the canny county of Cumberland, the land of rocks and mountains. We were still nine miles from Keswick, when the evening clouds began to hover over us, and the dark sides of the mountains, threw an additional gloom around.

We had sufficient light however, to enable us to see the road, and to guard against the rocky precipices on the edge of it, until we arrived at the Cherry Tree Tavern at Wythburn, a lonely house called Halfway House, between Ambleside and Keswick, and Matthew Jopson, the host here, is known by almost everyone who has travelled about the lakes.

Just after passing Dunmaile Raise, the first glance is caught of the hightly mountains of Skiddaw and Saddleback; but from the dustiness that prevailed, we were prevented from seeing these Monarch Mountains.

We had just a peep thro' the gloom, at the lake of Thirlmere, or as it is sometimes called Leathes Water or Wythburn Water; a lake more gloomy still than that of Rydal. The dim twilight was sinking into darkness, and:

> *Fast closed the shades of eve – the sun's last ray,*
> *That lingered sadly on the verge of day,*
> *Cast a wild spectral light, on sulphurous clouds,*
> *Careering past, like giants in their shrouds.*

Ere we were within six miles from Keswick, we were completely enveloped in darkness, and darkness too, of such a depth as completely precluded us from seeing either the rocks on our right hand, or the chasms on our left.

We none of us knew the road except Crosthwaite, and him we had not seen since we were at Matthew Jopson's; from which place our companion had started at full speed, determining, he said, to be at Keswick before us. We endeavoured in vain, when at Grasmere, to prevail upon our companion to keep up with us, for finding he had made rather too free use with the glass, we were fearful of his safety, if left alone.

His absence therefore, added considerably to our anxiety; his horse, moreover, was high-spirited, and he had experienced some difficulty in managing it. We were consequently as much alarmed on his account as our own.

Medcalfe every now and then exclaimed, "Oh! I do wish that Crosthwaite was with us!" or, "What shall I do if any misfortune should befall him, as is more than likely with such a horse, himself in such a state, on such a night, and on such a dangerous road!"

Then, "I should be forever be blamed by his relatives, for it was on my account that he came with me!"

And, "Gracious Heaven, what if his horse should have thrown him, and he

CROSSTHWAITE STARTED OFF AT FULL SPEED ON HIS METTLESOME MARE, FOR KESWICK.

W. M. STUART.

97

should be extended across the road and we run over him, I should never be forgiven!"

And added, "Oh! What if he should be dashed down a rocky precipice, or carried by his ungovernable horse over moss, or marsh, or quagmire!"

In this strain did my companion indulge for some time, and this tended no little to increase the unpleasantness of our situation.

We now moved on at a very slow pace, and left the horses to choose their path, for they could see in the dark far better than we could, and to guide them therefore, would be madness. Thus we travelled for a mile or two, at the rate of not more than three miles an hour. We met with no vehicle and it was hardly expected that we should; we overtook but a single person on the road, who, to console us, declared that the road was very good, but the pits on the side were "muckle steep!"

We could see neither the heavens above, nor the earth beneath; the mountains on the one hand and the precipices on the other, were equally imperceptible; the only objects that were occasionally visible were, now and then, a faint glimmering light from a shepherd's hut, or cottage on the hillside, at the distance of some two or three furlongs.

Thirlmere Bridge, looking north, 1833. T. Allom.

Every now and then Medcalfe was wondering what had become of Crosthwaite, the thought of whom still aggravated the more, our forlorn and dangerous situation. As Medcalfe and I were in advance of Yates and Hamilton, we were in the greatest danger, for we led the way for our companions behind, and if we had been thrown over the precipice they would receive warning, of course, not to follow.

Our fears being raised to the highest pitch, we stopped our gigs, to hold a sort of council of safety, and to consult what was best to be done, for the last two or three miles was at the hazard of our lives. To return to Grasmere was as dangerous as to proceed, and to remain stationary was not very desirable.

After deliberating for some time, it was resolved to go forward, and that we should get out of the gigs and lead the horses. We had not long acted upon this resolution, when we perceived at a distance before us, a brighter light than we had yet seen.

We could not, however, at first discover whether this light was at rest, or in motion, on the roadside or upon the mountain brow. It might be an *ignis fatuus* or a light proceeding from some shepherd's hut on the side of the hill. As we advanced however, the light became more distinct. It was stationary, and we were satisfied that it proceeded from a building of some sort or other on the roadside.

I have heard of the joy of a 'wayworn traveller' at reaching the end of a long and dangerous journey – I have read of the mariner, after a long voyage, how glad he is to see his native land again, and it is only by picturing in the imagination, the joys such as these, that you can form an adequate conception of the gladness that we experienced, at seeing this light by the side of the road.

We had now approached the isolated building from which the light gleamed. It was a smithy, and as we drew up to the door, the sound of our horses' feet, and the rattling of our carriages, brought a man to the threshold. It was evident that we could not take up our abode here for the night, nor were we very solicitous on that score, provided we could proceed in safety to Keswick. Our main object therefore, was to provide a safe conduct.

At first we conceived that a lamp would serve every purpose, and we asked the man at the smithy door if he would furnish us with such a thing. The man seemed rather embarrassed or worried at our enquiry, and whether he was doubtful of our honest intentions, failing to understand us or

'We now approached the isolated building...'   W. M. Stuart.

whatever else was the cause of his hesitation, I know not, but we waited some time for an answer.

During this suspense, another man made his appearance, whose dark features and leathern apron denoted him to be a son of Vulcan. To him we repeated the question, and from him we got a prompt reply, that he thought he could find us a Lanthorn, and he would immediately go and look for one.

During the absence of the smith, we learnt from the man whom we had first interrogated, that we were in the Vale of St. John, and this information recalled to my recollection some verses of Sir Walter Scott's, relative to this place, which I shall not omit to quote, as being suitable to our station, as well as descriptive of the place itself.

> *With toil, the traveller his way pursued,*
> *By lonely Threlkeld's waste and wood,*
> *Till on his course obliquely shone,*
> *The narrow valley of St. John,*

Piled in by many lofty a hill,
The narrow dell lay smooth and still;
And down its verdant bosom led
A winding brooklet found its bed.   Sir Walter Scott.

John Hutchinson, (for that was the name of the smith) soon returned with a Lanthorn, about the size of a watchman's, and now the question arose, as to where it should be placed, so as to throw the light to our front.

We fixed it in various positions, but all to no purpose, for the emitted rays, instead of lighting the path before the horse, created a dazzling light around us and rendered the road, a yard before us, quite imperceptible. This plan proving abortive, we struck a bargain with the blacksmith, to act as our guide and to carry the Lanthorn before us to Keswick.

Letter 12

Our new guide (John Hutchinson); singular night scene; carousel amongst the mountains; a song; our guide's loquacity; an enlivening prospect; arrival at Keswick; entertainment at the Queen's Head; evening festivities

Dear E...,

It took John about five minutes to make the necessary arrangements for his journey, and during this short interval he had been by no means idle, for he presented himself before us a new man.

He had cast off his leathern apron, and put on a short frock coat, which reached to his knees, a highland cap was placed loosely on his head, and a pair of stout built clogs graced his lowest extremities. He now had the appearance of a dapper little fellow, dressed and decorated for an amatory excursion.

The Vale of St. John, 1835.   G. Pickering.

There was one thing, however, which he seemed to have omitted in his preparations, in the application of a little soap and water to his face, which still presented the same sombre hue. But there was something in his look, which indicated a sharpness and intelligence, beyond what I should have expected to meet with, in a son of Vulcan, and a resident of St. John's Vale.

Thus equipped with Lanthorn in hand, our new guide advanced about twenty paces before us, and the signal, "All's right!" being given, we set off at a gentle trot after the nimble footed blacksmith. Our retinue had a most singular appearance. I could compare the light from the Lanthorn to nothing so like as a *Will-o-the wisp;* we proceeded for about a mile without stopping, our guide footing it all the way with astonishing agility.

Fearful of fatiguing him, however, we halted on the top of a hill, to give him some rest and refreshment, one of our party having a brandy bottle, (to which he gave the appropriate name of Pistol). He handed this to our guide, telling him to "charge and fire!" and John unhesitatingly obeyed the mandate, prefacing his charge with the following sentiment:

Long may ye live, and happy may ye be;
Blessed with contentment and prosperity.

THUS EQUIPPED WITH LANTHORN IN HAND, AND THE SIGNAL "ALL'S RIGHT!" BEING GIVEN, WE SET OFF.

W.M. STUART.

Nor was John the only one of our company that stood in need of the Pistol, for after the mental anxiety we had all of us laboured under, and the mountain air being chilly, we each of us took a little of the exhilarating beverage, to enliven our spirits, and to warm our frames.

Our spirits were revived, and the more to enliven us, we called upon our dark featured guide to give us a song. We had no sooner made the request than John doffed his cap and made a low bow, quite in the theatrical style, and sang the song of 'The Spider and The Fly' with such emphasis and action as quite astonished us. For its unusual content, I will here be your scribe, for you to judge its entertainment:

> *"Will ye walk into my parlour?" said yon spider to a fly;*
> *"Why, I'd like to very much, Sir," was the fly's polite reply.*
> *The fly sat down – the spider pounced, then gave a startled cry;*
> *For as he wildly staggered back, he heard his victim sigh,*
> *"I ken full well, ye canny fool, to eat me ye would try –*
> *The joke's on ye, because I am – a hand-made Fishing Fly!"*

What a scene we now presented! This was far different from any thing I ever witnessed before! Here was a party of tourists, upon a mountain top, under the canopy of a dark sky, with a figure before them, habited in a short surtout, holding a tartan cap in one hand, and a large Lanthorn in the other, singing with all the grace of an experienced comedian.

Such a singular spectacle did we exhibit, that I really believe that if any human creature had chanced to see us, whilst we were thus carousing, we should have been taken for something supernatural, but we were perfectly secure from intrusion, for the spot that we occupied, seldom, at such a time of night, would have heard the sounds of human footsteps.

The only objects there was any chance of disturbing, by our revels, were the spirits of the mountains, or the sheep; or if perchance a neighbouring rustic heard our mirthful songs, he might take us for a party of gypsies, and hasten away to secure his barn, or his harvest against our intrusion. Or if he was at all superstitious, he might bless himself as being within the range of the voices of the fairies; or he might think, perhaps, that the spirits of the Druids were moving amongst the mountains, for we were now not far from the spot where, some two thousand years ago, the Druids had a temple, and performed their rites.

John Hutchinson had quite ingratiated himself with us; and well he might,

Where the spirits of the Druids live. W. M. Stuart, 1982.

for he not only did his utmost to guard us, against the dangers that encompassed us, but he enlivened us on our journey, which seemed dark and dreary, as well as perilous. We kept the horses at an ambling pace, that John might not be tired. He trudged by our sides, and our slow movement gave him an opportunity of indulging in a little chitchat to which he evinced a strong desire. We cherished this inclination by an occasional drop of brandy, till at length our guide became quite garrulous.

He gave us, unsolicited, a history of his life, and account of his present circumstances. The former years, was not, indeed, much varied; he had not travelled far, nor had he been subject to many vicissitudes. He had at one time resided in Preston, and knew several persons there.

But in telling us of his present situation, there was one circumstance to which he was peculiarly anxious to draw our attention, and this was that he was, "The Master o' the smithy, and not the man, and I would not for any wee bit o' money," said he, "have it that any o' the farmers in the neighbourhood should spot me returning home after daybreak, for they would thus suspect I had been carousing in Keswick!"

Thus did our guide beguile the time of our dreary journey in the dark, now giving us a song, now a sentiment, and now a tale, in which he figured as the actor. At each mile-stone, he called out to appraise us that we were so much nearer Keswick, and when he announced that we had arrived at the last mile-stone, it was an intimation, as grateful to us, as is the watchman's call of the hour before sunrise to the sick man, who has been rolling restless upon his bed all night, wishing for daybreak.

By and by, we saw glimmering lights at a distance, apparently in a valley; and they increased in number and brilliancy, as we proceeded onward – they were the lights of Keswick, and we hailed them with exhilaration, as signs that our perilous journey was nearly at an end, and as signals of our approach to a place of rest and recreation.

We had just descended the high hill on this side of the town and arrived at the turnpike, when who should greet us but our friend Crosthwaite who, I have already told you, left us at Wythburn, and whose absence occasioned so much anxiety. To see him safe was an additional cause for gladness. He directed us to drive to the Queen's Head, at which he had provided accommodation for us.

Keswick, from the Ambleside road, 1840. S. Bough.

I can hardly describe the joy we felt on our arrival at the inn. You may form some faint idea, however, if you ever awaked out of a dream of perilous adventures, and rejoiced at finding yourself secure in a comfortable bed. The pleasure you then experience, at finding yourself safe from imaginary perils, may give you some slight notion of our joy, in finding ourselves safely brought to 'heaven' through real dangers.

After such a journey, the blazing hearth of the neat parlour of the inn, had a double charm, and the easy sofa was far more inviting than it was wont to be on ordinary occasions. The table soon groaned beneath the ponderous weight of a load of luxuries; there was plenty of ham, eggs, beef and tongue, then tea and coffee; and this was, in reality, one of the finest treats that I e'er sate down to devour. We were not so much engaged in taking care of ourselves, as to be unmindful of our friend the blacksmith.

We gave orders that he should regale himself in the kitchen, and that he should afterwards be introduced into the parlour. Then we should requite him for his services, and give him, moreover, something to cheer on his homeward journey; which you will remember, he dare not defer till daybreak, lest his Cumberland customers should suspect he had been 'Carousing at Keswick!'

In due time our guide was introduced; he seemed the better for the kitchen fare. He very politely doffed his cap as he entered the room, and we placed him in an elevated chair. He enlivened the evening by giving us a few of his best Cumberland songs, and we were much gratified by a sight of some of his drawings (for he was a artist) which were at the inn, and which did him infinite credit.

But the time was arrived for John to leave us, and on our settling with him, we offered to give him more than we had agreed to, but he positively refused to receive any further recompense, urging as argument for his refusal (what very few under similar circumstances would venture to interpose), that, "A bargain is a bargain." We treated him liberally however, and when the parting time came on, we all of us expressed ourselves highly pleased with the part he had taken, grateful for his services, and sorry at his departure.

The remainder of the evening was spent in talking about our night's adventures, which none of us, I am sure, will ever forget. And never did time appear to me to pass more rapidly, than it did from the period of our arrival at Keswick, to the time when the chambermaid was summoned to attend to the ablutions.

Letter 13

*Preparation for a morning walk; ascent of Castlehead; magnificent scene;
monumental seats; reflection; the town of Keswick; places of amusement;
church; inns and antiquities; remains of Druids Temple*

Dear E...,

The pranks of the previous day had taken such a stronghold in my thoughts,
that I could not sleep for some time after I retired to rest, and the consequence
was, that when I should have been up in the morning, I was still disposed to
slumber.

Thrice did I receive a summons to arise, ere I could muster resolution to
do so. But after the third tap at my chamber door, accompanied by a message
from the hoarse voice of the boots, that my friends were waiting for me, and
were about to walk out, I quickly dressed, and prepared to accompany them.

The morning was rather unfavourable; a hazy atmosphere and drizzling

Keswick, from Greta Bridge, 1833.   H. Castineau.

108

rain, were the first objects that attracted my attention on looking out of my chamber window. This was unfortunate, because at Keswick, above all other places, a clear atmosphere is the chief consideration of the tourist, to enable him to see in their full majesty, the lofty mountains of Skiddaw and Saddleback.

I found Medcalfe in the sitting room awaiting my arrival. Yates and Crosthwaite had sallied out; but as for Hamilton, he had not yet got release from the iron grasp of Morpheus, who, I suppose, kept him in durance, surely in consequence of not having sacrificed sufficiently at the shrine of the drowsy Deity, the night before.

Notwithstanding the unfavourable state of the weather, Medcalfe and I were soon in the open air, and as he had been at Keswick before, and knew something of the place and the scenery about it, I placed myself under his guidance. After progressing a short distance from the town, my companion led me over a stile into a plantation.

This plantation covers a large hill, which Medcalfe told me he had ascended on a former occasion, and that he should never forget the views from its summit as long as he lived. After hearing such a flattering account of the prospect from the top I said, "Let us ascend the hill, by all means. Lead the way, and I will follow!"

The ascent was not so difficult, because it was not so precipitous as that of the crag at Bowness, but tho' the acclivity was not so steep, yet the elevation was much higher. We had occasionally to rest on the way, and the views we had from the different points of our elevation were varied, extensive and interesting.

After a long and circuitous route we reached the top, and I soon found that my companion had by no means exaggerated the excellence of the prospect there from. Altho' the day was unpropitious for the view, in its fullest extent, yet we were gratified with a sight sufficiently magnificent, to requite the labour of a journey ten times as long and circuitous as the one that we had taken.

Immediatly before us, and apparently at no greater distance than a stone-throw, arose the mighty mountains of Skiddaw and Saddleback, loosing their lofty summits in the clouds. Volumes of mists were rolling down the sides of the hills, or hanging lazily in the ravines. On the right beneath us lay expanded the lake of Derwentwater, with rugged and stupendous rocks bordering it on one side, and the hills of Borrowdale on the other, the further

Keswick Lake, 1820. W. Westall, ARA.

point of the lake being obscured by the mist, and was lost to our view.

The hill whereon we stood, presented the appearance of a ruined fortress, and probably its name of Castlehead was taken from this similarity. The side opposite to that which we ascended, consisted of huge masses of perpendicular rocks, to look down which fills the mind with awe.

On the summit of the hill two rustic seats are raised, for the comfort and accommodation of visitors. Many a name was engraved thereon, of male and female, old and young, from all parts of the country, for some of the ages and places were attached to the names. Many a device, too, was there to be seen, some of which it was difficult to decipher. But the pierced heart and the pointed quiver evidently indicated that some aroused swain or lovesick maid had been there at work. From some of the dates, it would seem that these seats had withstood many a winter's blast.

It was curious to behold the diminutive appearance of the objects beneath us. The castle seemed as cottage, houses as huts, boats like seagulls – all seen like disguises, and if these objects appeared so diminutive from the position we occupied, how must they appear from the top of Skiddaw and Saddleback.

We observed two persons trudging through a lane, not very far from us;

and Medcalfe, whose eye could reach further than mine, recognised in these persons, our friends Yates and Crosthwaite. We hailed them, but our loudest shouts could not assail their ears, nor our repeated waving of handkerchiefs catch their eyes. They were making progress towards the town, and we therefore began our descent, expecting to meet them at the foot of the hill.

Nothing is more calculated to induce a train of serious and solemn reflection, than being placed upon the top of a high mountain. When the body is thus elevated, as it were, above the world, and the mind naturally participates in a corresponding elevation of sentiment, man cannot look down from an eminence upon the magnificent works of creation, without being led to look up to Nature's God; does the sceptic then ask, "Who is the Creator of what he sees before him?"

The silent eloquence of the surrounding scenery tells him that, no less than infinite wisdom and power could have planned and executed what he beholds, and can he do otherwise than adore the creator, for his goodness in providing these things, for man's use and enjoyment?

We overtook our companions ere we reached the town, into the streets of which we all paraded together. The town now presented a lively appearance, and we were told that there were a pretty fair number of visitors, but we did

The Market Square, Keswick, as it might have looked in 1840. W. M. Stuart.

not see many Lakers looking about them.

It so happens at the lakes, that you do not meet many strangers in the towns, the object of the tourists' attention being scattered over a large surface. The visitors are scattered accordingly, hence it is not there, as at fashionable watering places, where there are but few public promenades, upon which at one time of day or other, you may meet with almost everyone at the place. At the lakes, you meet perchance a tourist, like yourself, and when you have passed him, it is only a hundred to one chance that you may see him again. We never, for instance, saw again the dashing collegians, The Yorkshiremen, nor the gentleman who had travelled the world over.

I have already mentioned that Keswick is, as it were, the capital town of the Cumberland lake scenery. It may also be compared to a summerhouse in the midst of romantic gardens and pleasure grounds, to which the visitors enter for rest and refreshment, and from which they immerge, in all directions, some to one point of attraction and some to another – the painter in search of the picturesque, or the antiquarian directing his steps to the Temple of the Druids, whilst the mineralogist bends his course to the mountains, the

angler seeks the lake, and the lovers seek retirement in the grotto; and they that we admit to no classification, ramble at random, (and these compose by far, the greatest number).

Keswick is an ancient town, but it has something very attractive in its look. There are some modern built, neat and elegant houses, which are let to visitors ready furnished, and to amuse the company in unfavourable weather; there is an exhibition of drawings and paintings, principally of views of the lakes, and also a Museum of Fossils and Minerals, but we did not visit either the exhibition or the museum.

We passed Greta Hall, the elegant, yet hidden home of our Poet Laureate, Robert Southey, which was oft times frequented by William Wordsworth, and other illustrious poets; but we saw nothing of these gentlemen on our visit.

The church is a plain edifice, but there is one peculiarity about it, which I cannot help noticing and that is that a signpost of the museum was affixed upon its wall. The inns at Keswick are excellent and fitted up in the first style of that at which we put up, the Queen's Head. It is called 'Brougham's House', for he always stops there, and he was at the inn about a fortnight before we were. At Keswick, whether the sign of the Queen's Head is the cause or effect of this inn being the favourite of the Lord Chancellor, I cannot say, but another neighbourhood of Keswick possesses peculiar charms for the antiquarian.

It was anciently the resort of religious devotees, as well as those of the Dark Ages of our idolatrous ancestors, the Ancient Britons, as of the more modern ages of Christianity. The remains of the Druidical Temple are still to be seen at a short distance from Keswick, where at some fifteen hundred or two thousand years ago, the Druids held their courts, and performed their idolatrous rites and ceremonies.

You are perhaps aware that the Druids were Judges in civil affairs, as well as priests, and were eminent of the useful, as well as the cabalistic sciences. They were skilled in astronomy, arithmetic, mechanics, medicine, botany, rhetoric, magic, divination, and were also philosophers. I was sorry that I had not the opportunity of visiting the remains of the Druids' Temple, but it may not be uninteresting to give you a description of it, as I had it from others.

What is now seen of this Temple is a collection of about forty large stones, each from four to eight feet long, some upright and others prostrate, arranged in an oval shape, and forming an area of about 34 yards long, and 30 yards

Castlerigg Standing Stones, Keswick.   W. M. Stuart.

broad. This area encloses a lesser one. The larger is supposed to have been reserved for the inferior Druids who were numerous, and the lesser one, to have been set apart for the chief priests, who officiated at the sacrifices. Being in the vicinity of this monument of antiquity, my fancy busied itself and something like the following ideas floated in my mind.

I thought of the assembly of the Druids in their groves of oaks, for the oak, you know, was regarded by them as the emblem of the Almighty, and as his peculiar place of residence. I fancied I saw the priests marching in solemn procession, dressed in their long white surplices, their brows encircled with chaplets of oak leaves, their necks and wrists adorned with golden bracelets, and bearing wands in their hands. I imagined them searching for the mistletoe, which they foolishly fancied to contain a divine nectar, and to be the gift of Heaven.

I pictured in my imagination, the preparation of the sacrifice of the bulls, which they immolated, upon large stones strewn over with the leaves of the oak. The painful feeling which is exacted at contemplating such idolatrous superstition of our forefathers, is somewhat tempered by contrasting our situation with theirs.

Tho' we cannot help heaving a sigh over the memory of the poor benighted Druids and their ignorant followers, yet the very causes which prompt the sigh, leads us to rejoice in praises that our lot has been cast in a more enlightened age. I must crave your pardon for this digression – the subject was too tempting; I hope, however, that the train of thought to which a reflection upon the Druids Temple has given rise, may not be unprofitable, either to you or myself.

I have already intimated that the country of the lakes and mountains was a chosen retreat for religious devotees of the Christian era, as well as for the Druids.

The islands upon Keswick Lake, 1830.

This is apparent from the account, which we have of two of the islands upon the Keswick Lake, one of which is called the Vicars Isle, and is said to have formerly belonged to Fountains Abbey in Yorkshire. The other is called Herbert's Island, upon which the eminent recluse of that name, so far back as the seventh century, built a rude hermitage, wherein he lived and died, the remains of whom are supposed still to exist within the stone walls, which are visible to this day.

Letter 14

A drowsy companion; breakfast; the bonny boatman; lake guides;
Derwentwater; sail to Vicars Island; house of General Peachy;
Lords Isle; a tradition; Hamilton's singing; St. Herbert's Isle;
view of a distant waterfall; black lead mines.

Dear E...,

On our return to the inn, after our morning's ramble, we found Hamilton anxiously waiting our arrival. He had not, it seems, been long released from the thraldom in which we left him, and at the breakfast table, he began to evince a strong desire to be doing something. He had quitted the 'Temple of Morpheus' to pay his vows to 'Epicurus', and indeed we, one and all, to speak plain English, wished for breakfast, and we were not long in having our wishes consummated. I feel sure that our host would not profit much by this *dejeuner*, especially as it respected to such as us, as had breathed the morning air from the top of Castlehead so early in the morning.

We arranged over our repast that, as soon as it was ended, we would have a sail upon the lake, and in less than an hour, we found ourselves trudging by the side of our boatman to the banks of Derwentwater, or the Keswick lake.

The boatman was a man of hale and handsome features, good, partly teasing, insinuating address, and intelligent conversation. And as he is the last guide we had occasion for, in this our tour, I cannot, in taking leave of our lake guides, omit to mention that they, in general, possess a knowledge not limited, as one may be supposed, to an acquaintance only of the country and the people within the sphere of their peregrinations, but a knowledge of men and things in general. I was astonished at many of the remarks made by our old boatman of Windermere, the guide on Curwen's Island, by the honest smithy, Hutchinson, and by our sharp-eyed, handsome boatman of Derwentwater.

Having arrived at the boat, and being comfortably seated upon downy cushions, splash went the oars, and softly did we glide upon the silvery

Derwentwater from Castlehead, Cumberland, 1832. T. Allom.

streams of Derwentwater. Before I proceed further, I will mention a circumstance connected with this lake that may not be uninteresting to you.

From the name of the lake, the family of Radcliffe took their title, of the Earls of Derwentwater. They had large possessions here, held a castle upon Castlerigg, a short distance from Keswick, and a house upon what is now become an island on the lake, but the site of which was, at that period, a peninsula. The downfall of this family, you know, is a subject of English history.

The last Earl, unfortunately attaching himself to the cause of the last of the Stuarts, marched at the head of the Jacobite Army to Preston in 1715 and was, at the siege of my native town, taken prisoner, conveyed to London, tried and beheaded, on Tower Hill. His estates were confiscated, and those of them in the neighbourhood of the lake, which we were now traversing, were given to the trustees of Greenwich Hospital, who still hold them.

The scenery about Derwentwater is far different from that of Windermere; the latter is eminently beautiful, the former magnificently sublime – that of Windermere is composed of sloping lawns, hanging woods and pretty pastures, whilst that of Derwentwater consists of tremendous rocks and lofty mountains – Windermere is rendered lively by rustic villas, handsome mansions, smiling meadows, and elevated Observation Stations, but Derwentwater presents a solemn appearance, having but few houses and meadows upon its banks. It is a scene of solitary seclusion and grand magnificence.

View of Derwentwater from Vickers Isle, 1774. W. Bellers.

The day being overcast, it threw an additional solemnity over the scene, and had it not been for the hilarity of our crew, I verily believe I should have fallen into a deep despondency, so well calculated was the scene before me to induce such a mood. We had not been long upon the lake, before we were overtaken by a shower, but having taken precaution, on leaving Keswick, to guard against such an event, we were not much the sufferers from it. The rain was neither heavy nor of long continuance, and it was again quite fair ere we reached Vicars or Derwent Isle.

In sailing under the dark side of this island, the trees upon its border were almost as distinctly perceptible in mirrored form, on looking at the water as they were above it. Our boatman told us that we were now upon the deepest part of the lake, and that a few years ago, a fatal accident happened here to a party of sportsmen who, whilst the lake was frozen over, had been too venturesome.

This island contains about six acres of land. I have already told you that it once belonged to Fountains Abbey, and perhaps it was then occupied by some of those possessed Ecclesiastics of that establishment who had renounced all sublunary enjoyments, bid farewell to the world, and devoted themselves, *Secum esse et secum vivare.*

The island now has upon it a handsome house, belonging to General Peachy – how changed now is the place both as to its tenants and tenement – once the abode of the peaceful anchorite, now the residence of a warlike General; once containing a solitary cell, on the site of which now rises a beautiful mansion.

In some degree, however, the silent seclusion of the spot is yet maintained, and ever will be, and I cannot but admire the taste of the present possessor, in selecting such a quiet retreat from the turmoil of his professional life.

Our boat, being drawn to the shore, we disembarked, and were conducted through the grounds towards the house by the boatman. The island rises rather precipitously from the lake, and so embowering are the trees and shrubs, that the General's house is not perceptible until you nearly approach it.

Overview of Derwentwater from the west. Photograph W. M. Stuart, 2006.

The walks of Derwent Isle differ from those of Curwen's Isle, just as those of a garden differ from those of a grove – here we were surrounded and overhung by shrubs, our pathway was decorated with flowers, and the spreading branches of the tulip tree was suspended over the walk; whereas on Curwen's Isle we walked thro' shady avenues of tall trees, which shot their perpendicular trunks towards heaven, and was lined with brushwood, and the old Hugo oak exhibited his bulky trunk, extending his gigantic arms around.

We approached the mansion by a winding footpath and came suddenly in front of it. I cannot call it a noble, tho' it certainly is a beautiful building – whether it is of stone or brick, I cannot tell you, for it was almost covered with trees, shrubs and flowers. At the door (before which, there is a portico of rustic latticework) we were met by one of the female domestics, who courteously invited us into the house. My friends, however, declined the invitation, alleging that as our time was limited, we had better advance up the lake, in order to see as much of the scenery about it as we could.

We therefore proceeded to the boat, and embarked once more upon the limpid lake of Derwentwater. The day was now fair, but not fine. The clouds still hung upon the hills, tho' not so heavily as they did on our first setting out from Keswick. A bright cloud occasionally smiled over us, and now and then a ray of the sun darted athwart a rock, or tipped the top of a distant mountain.

I cannot imagine a more beautiful sight than that which is caused by the playfulness of the sunbeams upon a mountain brow, shining over the wilderness of mists below, and chasing, as it were, the clouds from their resting places. Such a sight was particularly gratifying to us in as much as, it was a sign that fine weather was approaching.

These occasional glimpses of the sun seemed to animate our crew. The objects now round us wore a most lively aspect, and we skimmed gaily along the eastern side and towards the head of the lake. When we came near anything of remark, our guide, the boatman, was sure to point it out, and his expressive features as he made his statement, and his simple, yet earnest mode of making it, was sure to arrest our attention.

"That Island on your right, Gentlemen," said he, pointing to an island which we were passing, "is Lords Island, so called from its being formerly possessed by the Earls of Derwentwater, who had a house upon it."

Then he continued, "It is said that a drawbridge once reached from this island to that projecting part of the shore on your left." This tradition about the drawbridge, however, is rather apocryphal, for the better opinion is that Lords Island was formerly on a peninsula, in which case, a drawbridge would be unnecessary.

Our friend Crosthwaite here called our attention to a deep ravine in a huge rock on the shore.

"That," said the boatman, "is the spot where, it is said, Lord Derwentwater lay for weeks, hiding from the pursuit of his enemies, and through yonder glen, on the opposite shore, it is also said that his Countess made her escape, on hearing that her husband was taken prisoner."

Here a dead pause ensued, as if we were, all of us, instantly thinking of the sad effects of that unfortunate rebellion which caused to be struck off the last Lord Derwentwater's head, and his patrimonial estates to be taken from his family.

I know not how long this pause might have lasted had not Hamilton (who was in a merrier mood than to reflect upon the downfall of the Derwentwater family) suddenly strung his vocal lyre, to give us one of his Caledonian songs. I would observe of his singing that his assortment of songs is not very

The Lowdore waterfall, 1816. J. Farington.

121

new or numerous, and we were therefore more than once, in the course of our journey, favoured with *Auld Lang Syne* and *Bonny Brae*, but what our songster lacked in novelty and variety, he made up by his animated style, and above all by his merry Tam-o-Shanter style countenance, which well characterised the sentiments of the jovial fellowship contained in his favourite songs.

Our guide next pointed to an island at a considerable distance from us, being about at the middle of the lake, and told us that was St. Hubert's Isle. I have already mentioned this and as we did not pass near it, our eyes were soon withdrawn from it to another interesting object, vis a cascade gushing down from stupendous rocks at the distance of about half a mile before us, and towards which we were sailing.

This was Lodore Waterfall. The ethereal blue of the water, pencilled upon the dark brown rock, and falling from a considerable height, apparently in the bosom of the trees beneath, was a sight truly magnificent – a scene mixed up, of the beautiful and the sublime. So abounding is the lake of Derwentwater with interesting objects that you have scarcely fixed your eye upon one, than it is withdrawn to another.

The next thing to which our boatman claimed our attention was an object beneath, or rather *beneath the water,* and you will perhaps, be no less astonished than I was at being told that we were now sailing *over* an island. Think not, my dear boy, that this is an American story – I assure you, it is a fact.

The island of which I am speaking, was then under water. But it occasionally rises to the surface and appears for several weeks, and sometimes for months together, then it sinks again. Its visits above the surface are not frequent, however, and it has appeared but seven times or thereabouts, within the last thirty years. The clearness of the water enabled us to see distinctly, the light green grass, with which the island was covered.

This is one of those phenomena of nature, which baffles the ingenuity of man to account for. Our guide informed us that a few years ago he took to the island, a professor from one of the universities, who tried several experiments upon it, and by boring to a considerable depth, extracted a quantity of gas. And our philosophical boatman attributed to the gas, the periodical rise of the island, and to this he also attributed the 'underwinds', as they are called, which are occasional currents of air under the water of this lake, and which, when in motion, cause great difficulty in rowing or steering the boat.

The mountains south of Derwentwater.

Whether our guide's conclusions were right or not, I leave to others to judge, for I won't hazard an opinion on the subject.

My attention, being directed to the water, was fixed there for some time in regarding the pellucid stream, and the reflection of the rocks in it. So clean was the water, that we could see for many yards the pebbles, rushes and grasses, and plants at the bottom, and it was an interesting sight to see the fishes, when disturbed by the agitation of the water, retreating in all directions.

Every now and then, one of this shiny tribe, more hardy than the rest, would approach very near the boat, and remain motionless there for some time. He might be a messenger sent by his tribe, to ascertain whether we were friends or fishermen, and by his sudden darting downwards, it would seem as if he flew to tell his colleagues the results of his reconnoitring.

Our attention was next called to some hills, which were before us. Amongst these were the black lead mines, as noted throughout England. Here our friend Medcalfe, who had been for a long time silent (and I could not help suspecting, by the by, that his silence arose from thinking more about Kendal cottons, than Keswick Lake), interposed, to give us a piece of information.

"Those mines," said he, "have not been worked for some time. In fact I believe the skein is lost, and tho' several attempts have been made to regain it, yet the attempts have proved abortive. You would suppose," continued our mercantile companion, "that black lead pencils could be had much cheaper at Keswick than elsewhere, but the fact is otherwise, for I have even bought them for less at Birmingham, than I have got them for at Keswick. This is not an uncommon thing in trade, for you frequently meet with goods much cheaper at a distance from the place of manufacture, than at the place itself."

Letter 15

Landing at Lodore; the inn; the vale; the echo; the cannon and the cascade; adjournment to the inn; important deliberations there; a conflict of feelings; a grand view of the lake; an imprudent companion.

Dear E...,

After sailing a short way up the River Derwent, the most 'limpid and colourful' stream in this county, we came nearly opposite to the cascade, a distant view of which we had from the lake. The waterfall was not now in sight, being concealed behind some overhanging woods. Our boatman drew up to the shore where we debarked on a meadow, in front of the Lodore Inn.

This inn bears the name of Stephenson's Arms, and belongs to the family of Bowland Stephenson, who lately made such a noise in the banking world. It is romantically situated at the foot of Stephenson's Rocks. We caught a glimpse of its white-washed front for a considerable distance on the lake, and it presented a

Stephenson's Arms, Derwentwater.
Old photograph at the Lodore Hotel.

125

beautiful contrast to the long range of dark rocks behind it. So completely does this vale appear to be lined with rocks that I was, for some time, at a loss to conceive where the pass of inland communication could be.

We had advanced about twenty yards over the meadows, our guide lingering behind, as we thought for the purpose of fastening his boat to the shore, when our ears were assailed by a loud shout of, "Echo!" and no sooner was the shout raised, than the rocks reverberated the sound, at least a half a dozen times. We found that the shout proceeded from our boatman, whose object in keeping behind us was it seems, to surprise us in this agreeable manner. The keynote being given, we each of us in turn tried the power of our voices. All sorts of long and hard sounding names were vociferated, and the rocks threw back the sounds upon our ears with the utmost fidelity, and lost not a syllable. Yates tried his skill at his favourite word, "Santeradoodle," and "Santeradoodle" rebounded from rock to rock; and the hills, after reiterating the word fully at first, and nearly so a second time, afterwards muttered the concluding syllables less distinctly, and, "Doodle, oodle, oodle" died upon the ear in softer and still softer cadences.

Near the spot of our vocal exhibitions, a large cannon was placed, for the amusement of such as chose to be at the expense of hearing the sound of *its*

View of Derwentwater from above the Lodore Falls. W. Westall, ARA.

echo. We, however, were quite satisfied with the echo of our own voices, and the charge for 'charging the cannon' being rather high, we preferred hearing the sound of our silver jingling in our pockets to that of the cannon's roar.

Having gratified our ears with the echoes, we bent our course towards the cascade, there to satisfy our sight with the waterfall. The sound of the cascade now began to be audible. Passing over the meadow, we proceeded through a garden, which adjoins the inn, and advanced along a pasture field, at the end of which we arrived at a woody glen, where a clear stream flowed over a bed of bright pebbles. The trees now began to thicken around us, and the sound of the cataract was heard more distinctly. It was as the sound of distant thunder, and became fainter and fainter as it rolled along the rocks.

We had, now and then, a partial glance of the cascade, thro' the branches of the trees. After traversing the side of the meandering stream for some distance, we came at length in view of a rustic wooden bridge, and we had at the same time a full view of the waterfall in all its grandeur.

And how shall I describe it! I must confess my inability to do so, and must content myself with simply telling you that there fell before us a mass of water from an elevation of 150 feet, not in one continuous sheet however, but in columns of several yards each in height. What a grand scene this must be, when the water forms one continual and unbroken sweep, from the top to the bottom, as is the case after heavy rain. The rocks, between which the torrent swept its impetuous course, raised their points to a tremendous height on each side of the fall. One of these rocks, called the Shepherd's Crag, rises to an elevation of five hundred feet. The water came tumbling down with an overwhelming force from rock to rock.

In one impetuous torrent, down the steep,
It thundering shoots, and shakes the country round.
An azure sheet, it rushes broad, with power –
Then whitening by degrees, as prone it falls,
And on the loud resounding rocky ground,
Dashed in a cloud of foam, it sends aloft
A hoary mist, which forms a ceaseless shower –

Yates and I advanced to the foot of the fall, and left our companions behind, who were content to view it at a greater distance. Here the noise was

The Lodore Cataract, 1833. T. Allom.

so astounding that I could not hear the voice of my companion, bawled he ever so loudly. So loud indeed, is the roar of the cataract that sometimes, so travellers say, it has been heard at the distance of a dozen miles. The echo from the surrounding hills contributes much to the increase of sound.

The basin formed by the fall of the water was very deep and clear as crystal. The stream from the pool at first rushes in agitated confusion, but afterwards steals, in silent seclusion, along the 'rude sequestered vale' to the River Derwent.

High above our heads rose tremendous precipices. Branches of trees stretched themselves across the ravine and formed a shady bower. The sides of the rocks exhibited a vast variety of hues; here a clayey brown, there a deep green, here covered with verdure, and there with hanging wood; in one place the moss clinging to the sides, in another, the roots of trees spreading themselves in all kinds of fantastic shapes. The light blue vault of the sky crowned the whole, and the spreading branches seemed as if they were drawn upon the cerulean firmament –

Beside this dewy border, let me sit,
All in the freshness of the humid air,
There, in that hollow root, grotesque and wild,
An ample chair, moss lined, and overhead,
By flowering umbrage, shaded pattern shed –

We spent some time in viewing this cataract, and then adjourned to Stephenson's Arms, where, over our pot of porter, we deliberated as to our future course. It was then Thursday. Our Kendal friends could not spend with us more than that day, and Hamilton was required to be at home the following evening. With respect to Yates, it was not absolutely necessary for him to be at home until Saturday, and as for myself I was not, within a few days required either to return.

The question was therefore with Yates and myself, "Shall we go on to Ullswater, or return with our companions?" I need not detail to you the arguments pro and con, but will merely state the result. The unfavourable state of the weather induced us to abandon all thoughts of further progress, and we therefore determined to accompany our friends on their homeward journey.

I must confess that no sooner had we come to this resolution than I felt sad

Skiddaw in the sunset, 1787. P. J. Loutherbourg.

129

– sad at the thought of quitting scenes that I so much delighted to gaze upon. This feeling is a common one. A tourist of pleasure generally feels a regret at returning, but then the sorrow which it occasions, is met by the joyous thought of home, so that a conflict of opposite passions is going on about him, like clouds contending with sunshine on an April day. I heaved a sigh at contemplating my departure from the fairy scenes of Cumberland and Westmorland, but I was consoled, by thinking that I did so, to enjoy the sweets of home.

We left the romantic vale of Lodore about eleven o'clock, and in little less than an hour we reached the point from which we started on our aquatic excursion. I must not, however, thus hastily hurry you back to Keswick, without noticing the delightful prospect or two, which we had on our return.

The majestic front of Skiddaw arose before us, and his dark and rugged features seemed to scowl upon the lesser hills around him, whilst the white houses of Keswick formed a lively contrast to the sombre hues of the hills behind it. The distant view of Crosthwaite Church, to the left of Keswick gave an additional interest to the scene, which was still more heightened by the neat house of Southey, the Poet Laureate, which was just perceptible

A view near Keswick, 1787. F. Wheatly.

beyond the racecourse.

During our sail back to Keswick, Yates, in one of those fanciful freaks which are sometimes indulged in, in opposition to prudence, would doff his coat, and try his skill at the oar; an exercise unobjectionable, indeed, when taken at a fitting time, but highly improper at this period, as there was upon the lake, a very cold breeze, which would ill accord with the heat, which the exercise of rowing would occasion.

Notwithstanding our remonstrance, Yates persisted in his foolish determination, and he had to pay for his imprudence, with a cold which it engendered, and which he did not get rid of for several days. So fatigued was he, moreover, with his exercise, that he was as if he had lost the use of his limbs; and, as he observed, "He hardly knew whether or not he had all his bones about him".

Being once more at Keswick, which by our resolution at Lodore, was to be the ultimate point of our present excursion, we began to prepare for our homeward journey.

Letter 16

*Departure from Keswick for home; unexpected meeting with an artist;
view from Castlerigg; wild mountain scenery; a farewell; Helvellyn;
a tragical story; the gloomy vale of Thirlmere; melancholy*

Dear E...,

Everything ready, baggage packed, horses harnessed, bills paid, and all the
'What you please' gentry remunerated, we set off from Keswick a little after
twelve o'clock. We had not got quite out of the town when perceiving a person before us, walking at more than ordinary speed, I observed to Yates that
the man before us was very like W..., the artist from Preston.[1]

"The very same," rejoined my companion, "and he passed thro' Kendal
when we were there."

Greta Hall and Keswick Bridge, Cumberland, 1835.   W. Westall, A.R.A.

1 William Westall A.R.A. 1781-1850, from Preston.

132

We soon came up to the pedestrian, and it turned out that our conjecture was correct. So we two slowed ourselves to talk to him.

"Well W...., you are in search of the picturesque?" said I.

"Yes," he replied, "you perceive that we artists are obliged to trudge on foot, whilst you can drive your vehicles. Here I am rambling from lake to lake, with pencils and colours in my pocket."

He gave us a short account of his tour, which had been just of the same duration as ours, tho' in a contrary direction. " I always select this time of year," said he, "because now the tints are by far the finest and most suitable for the artist."

He was bending his course towards Ullswater, which lake he considered afforded the most abundant repast for the painter, but the day being hazy, this somewhat dampened his spirits, and he doubted whether to proceed to Ullswater or not. The artist walked alongside of us till we reached the summit of Castlerigg, when, pointing to an open country road on our left, he was about to turn his steps thitherwards, so we therefore took leave of him and soon reached our companions.

From the top of Castlerigg, which we had now attained, a most extensive prospect presents itself when the day is clear, but the dense state of the atmosphere prevented our enjoying a scene so delightful. We could just perceive, however, through the mist, the glassy surface of Derwentwater and the towering tops of Skiddaw and Saddleback.

We were now in the immediate vicinity of the Druids Temple of which I have already spoken, and I entertained a strong desire to visit the place, but the state of the weather (for it was now raining), and the anxiety of my companions to speed on their journey, stood opposed to my inclination.

St. John's Vale, 1997.

However, as the interest of the spot consisted entirely in the associations, which it excited in the mind of the beholder, perhaps those associations were as much excited in me, at the thought of being near the place, as they would have been, if I were at the place itself.

Ere we reached St. John's Vale, the sky began to brighten, and casting off our topcoats and throwing aside our umbrellas we had a better opportunity of regarding the 'Savage Scenery' wherewith we were encompassed.

This sort of scenery was novel to us; the hills on our right and left presented a rude and broken appearance. Large tracts of heath lay between us and the mountains, numerous flocks of sheep were browsing on the hilltops, and so diminutive did these appear, that they were scarcely distinguishable from the stones, which lay scattered about them.

A shepherd's hut was here and there to be seen, upon the side of the hill. It was from some of these that we had perceived the glimmering lights the night before. There were several small cascades falling from the hills, the sky-blue streams of which contributed greatly to the interest and variety of the mountain scenery.

On passing the smithy of John Hutchinson, that honest fellow shewed his dark features at the door, and I daresay whenever he hears the sound of horses' footsteps, he is led instinctively to the threshold. Having ascertained that he got home in safety and not long before daybreak, for which he was so solicitous, we took leave of our nocturnal guide, and perhaps for ever. But never shall I think of St. John's Vale, much less shall I visit that romantic spot, without being reminded of our nightly adventures there.

We travelled for some time without witnessing any material variation in the scenery. We had, however, an opportunity of measuring the danger, in which we were placed the night before, and grateful aught we to be to Him, for guiding us in safety, over a road, at every step over which, we incurred the risk of being precipitated headlong into the depths below, or dashed to pieces against the projecting rocks.

We now approached the foot of the mighty Helvellyn, which we had not an opportunity of seeing before (having passed it in the night), but which we now saw in all its rugged grandeur and wild magnificence. It is somewhat higher than Skiddaw, tho' it does not appear so, for the same reason, that a

Thirlmere and Helvellyn, looking south, 1833. T. Allom.

robust man does not look as tall as a spare one, altho' he may be in fact, the taller of the two.

The mind of the beholder is filled with a feeling of solemn awe, at looking upon this mighty mass of matter, and he is naturally led to reflect upon that vast convulsion of nature which cast so huge a mass together. The mountain presented a sterile appearance; its dark sides were here and there, however, enlivened with patches of verdure, a few straggling sheep, and a streamlet or two running down the ravines. The summit was invisible to us, and is, indeed, never to be seen by the traveller from the road, which we were passing over; and this is owing to the head of the mountain arising abruptly, as it were, from a pair of shoulders.

In regarding the tremendous declivities of the rocks of Helvellyn, the tourist, who has read Wordsworth's poetical account of *The Melancholy State of Charles Gouch,* cannot help heaving a sigh at the remembrance of the disastrous story, and the eye of the traveller endeavours to trace the scene of the tragical occurrence. As you may not have heard the tale, I will just give you the outlines of it; and the narration may, perhaps, contribute to increase the interest of the scenery as I take you with me along the foot of the mountains.

It was one morning early in the spring of 1805, that Charles Gouch, a young Cumbrian, had occasion to take a journey from Patterdale to Wythburn. The mighty Helvellyn lay between the two places, and Charles, being doubtless anxious to cut the journey short, resolved, it seems, to travel by the mountain pass, and his sole companion was his favourite dog. Ere Charles had completed his task of surmounting the hill, he was overtaken by a heavy fall of snow, which rendered trackless the mountain pass. The unwary traveller, missing his footing, was precipitated from the rocks above to the ravine beneath.

Days and weeks passed on, and Charles was neither seen nor heard of, nor was his dog to be found. After a lapse of three months, the body of the unfortunate youth was discovered by a shepherd, in a deep glen of the mountain, but what renders this story still more notable is the fact that when the corpse was discovered, the faithful dog was discovered also, watching over the lifeless remains of its master, and still uttering, in funeral screams, its piteous moaning.

Wordsworth has thus beautifully described this circumstance:

A barking sound the shepherd hears,
A cry as of a dog or fox
He halts, and searches with his eyes
Amongst the scattered rocks –
It was a cove, a huge recess
That keeps till June, December's snow.
A lofty precipice in front
A silent tarn below –

Far in bosom of Helvellyn,
Remote from public road or dwelling,
Pathway or cultivated land,
From trace of human foot or hand,
There sometimes does a leaping fish
Send thro' the tarn a lonely cheer.
The crags repeat a Raven's croak
In sympathy austere.

Thither the rainbow comes – the cloud
And mists that spread the flying shroud,
And sunbeams, and the sounding blast,
That if it could, would hurry past
But that enormous barrier binds it fast,
Not free from boding thoughts awhile,
The shepherd stood, then makes his way
Towards the dog, o'er rocks and stones
As quickly as he may.

A human skeleton on the ground.
The appalled discoverer, with a sigh,
Looks round to learn the history.
From those abrupt and perilous rocks
The man had fallen – that place of fear
At length upon the Shepherd's mind,
It breaks, and all is clear.

Nor far had gone before he found,
He instantly recalled the name,
And who he was, and whence he came;
Remembered too, the very day
On which the traveller passed that way.

But here a wonder, for whose sake
This lamentable tale I tell,
A lasting monument of words
This wonder merits well.

The dog, which still was hovering nigh
Repeating the same horrid cry
The dog had been thro' three months
space
A dweller in that savage place.

W. M. Stuart.

137

Yes, proof was plain, that since the day
On which the traveller thus had died,
The dog had watched about the spot
Or by his Master's side.

How nourished here thro' such long time,
He knows, who gave that Love sublime;
And gave that strength of feeling great,
Above all human estimate.

The melancholy thoughts of the tourist, occasioned by reflecting upon the mournful fate of Charles Gouch, are still heightened by the gloomy scenery, which meets his eye as he passes the mountain.

Not far from here flows the solitary lake of Thirlmere, or as it is sometimes called Leathes Water, or Wythburn Water; a dark, deep and gloomy lake extending itself for about three miles, between high, rugged and precipitous rocks, and barren, heath-covered hills. There is nothing indeed, to enliven

Leathes Water or Wythburn Water, 1833. G. Pickering.

138

the scene, neither house, cottage, wood or meadow. The only trees, which graced the banks, were a few tall firs, and these, instead of adding a little liveliness to the prospect, tended still more to increase its deep solemnity.

What a scene for grave reflection! What a spot for serious contemplation! What a retreat for the lover of melancholy! In bidding adieu to this place and to the recollections, which it raised, I do so in the words, and in perfect accordance with the sentiments of Henry Kyske-White who says:

"Tho' the scenes which I survey be mournful, and the ideas they excite equally sombre, though the tears gush, as I contemplate them, and my heart feels heavy with the sorrowful emotions which they inspire, yet they are not unaccompanied with sensations of the purest and most ecstatic!"

> *There is a kindly mood of melancholy,*
> *That wings the soul, and points her to the skies.*   Dyer.

Letter 17

The return; Dunmail Raise; Grasmere; Ambleside; Low Wood;
Troutbeck Bridge; Ings Chapel; Staveley; boors revelling;
arrival at Kendal; treaty for a horse; departure from Kendal;
Bolton-le-Sands; sportsmen; Lancaster; Garstang; home.

Dear E...,

I have now almost brought you to the termination of my tour, at least of that part of it which can be interesting to you, if any part of it can. After we passed the foot of Helvellyn, the road we traversed was that which we had passed over the day before, and as I have already spoken of the scenery along it, anything I might say now, would be but useless repetition. Suffice it to

STAVELY
IN 1803

W.M. STUART.

say, therefore, that the day now began to brighten, and our ride was delightful.

We passed Dunmaile Raise about three o'clock, and in less than half an hour afterwards, we were once more arrived at the romantic vale of Grasmere. Here we proposed to dine. The rate of charges at the Swan did not tempt us thither, however, and we drove to the Red Lion, an inn by the roadside, where, at a short notice, our hostess provided a plenteous supply of substantial fare, consisting of ham and eggs for the first course, and class cake and butter for the second; though our fare was humble, yet we made a hearty meal.

We arrived at Ambleside about six o'clock, but it was not meet that we should stop there, as we were but fourteen miles from Kendal, which place we were desirous of reaching, if possible before dark. We therefore drove through this town, and after passing the Low Wood Inn, turned off to our left, instead of proceeding to Bowness, and took the way past Troutbeck Bridge, Ings Chapel, and Staveley.

On approaching the last named place, we were astonished at the number of drunken men we met on the road, some reeling from one side of the lane to the other, and some prostrate. We ascertained at Staveley that there had been a Cattle Fair there that day, and I suppose that the farmers had washed down their bargains rather too freely with strong potations.

We stopped at Staveley about ten minutes to water the horses, and a scene was there exhibited, far different from what we had been accustomed to witness on our journey, and the contrast may perhaps be a sufficient apology for my mention of it. We chanced to step into a building adjoining the inn, used ordinarily, I should suppose, for the brewhouse, but fitted up as a temporary accommodation for the rustics who came to the fair.

In this place some fifty or sixty men and women were drinking, smoking, singing, bawling, and quarrelling. There was no fireplace, but upon the hick-covered floor of the apartment, some blazing faggots were heaped together, the smoke from which, mixing with fumes of tobacco, made its way through a round hole in the roof of the building. The only light by which we could see this strange group of revellers, was the fire on the floor, and this cast such a hue upon their features, as gave them a strange and tarterean appearance.

The remaining five miles of our journey to Kendal we had to travel in the dark, but this was nothing compared with our journey the night before, inas-

Bridge over the River Kent, Kendal (detail), 1833. T. Allom.

much as we were now upon an excellent road, every inch whereof was known to our Kendal companions; whereas then, we were traversing a way unknown to any of us, and at every advance over which, we were in peril of our lives.

Every now and then we were saluted with a hearty, "Good Night" from the passers by, and we arrived at Kendal in perfect safety, and without any further encounter about eight o'clock. We made ourselves known to the

Some text from Isaac's last letter from the Lake District.

innkeeper, then gave our trusty steed into the safekeeping of the ostler, who ungirt the gig, and attended to the animal's needs.

After enjoying a goodly repast we were not long before repairing to our chambers for the night. As the tourist is said never to have completed his narrative till he has brought himself back to his domestic circle, so it is perhaps fitting that I should add a few words upon our last day's journey. I shall be very brief in this, for I have not subject matter to be lengthy.

You must know then that the morning of our setting off from Kendal was very fine. It was one of those mellow harvest mornings, when the sharp air betokens the presence of a slight frost, and the bright sunbeams shining upon the grass, exhibit the dewdrops in pearly brightness. It was such a morning as makes the heart of the huntsman rejoice, tho' not for the same reason. I arose before my companions, and took a solitary ramble. Having passed the church, which bye the bye, they are always building, and has somewhat of a cathedral-like appearance, I perambulated the banks of the rapid flowing River Kent.

On my return to the inn along the banks of this river, I perceived near the northern bridge, a group of persons assembled, and my curiosity having induced me to the spot, whom should I discover as one of the principal persons in the group but my friend Yates.

"..... ATTEMPTING TO BARGAIN FOR A PONY."

My friend was bargaining or attempting to bargain for a pony. Much time was spent in the treaty, and spent in vain, for after the tedious ceremony of running the horse to and fro, examining its hoofs and knees, and teeth, inquiring into its age, birth, character, and disposition, the treaty broke off abruptly when the price came into question.

I will not detain you by describing the leave-taking of our friends at Kendal, suffice it to say that we left Kendal at eleven o'clock in the morning and after a delightful ride, arrived at Bolton-by-the-Sands about two o'clock, where we dined handsomely. On our

Preston and the Itinerant. W. Orme, 1796.

way to Lancaster we saw several sporting parties, some engaged in shooting, and others in coursing, and one hare we saw unseated, pursued and killed.

We drove through Lancaster without stopping there, and by the time we reached Garstang, the sun had gone down. We arrived at Preston at about eight o'clock, and found that all was well at home, where we were cordially welcomed in. We continue to this day to gratify our friends with telling them of some incident or other of our week's tour.

Epilogue, 1831-2008
The march of time - with some historical comments

I have set out to rediscover the journey that Isaac Simpson took so many years ago, and my overall impressions have been that in this north western region, whilst the buildings have largely survived, and the canny and friendly Cumbrian people and dialects are little changed, most of the alterations are associated with the need for speed in travel, and the effects of twentieth century mechanical advancements.

The gigs and sturdy horses so essential for travelling, and the men skillful in driving and handling their chariots have now faded into history, as have the ostlers in their stables at the many inns, and the blacksmiths, so necessary for long distance travel at that time. We have been left with the legacy of many delightful inns still in existence, mostly about twenty to thirty miles apart along the major routes, the distance considered a reasonable ride before resting one's horse. Milestones or posts became compulsory in 1767, because travel by coach was then charged by miles travelled.

Most people, who had the means and a good horse or two, visited their friends, and neighbouring towns within perhaps a radius of no further than approximately forty miles, allowing for time to return. We forget now the restrictions of horse travel and the poorly made roads of that time upon which the horses and gigs were subjected to travelling in all weathers. These faithful animals, so essential to man, faded out for all general use in the twentieth century, when cars gradually became more widely used after World War Two.

I set off in the autumn on this journey, in my comfortable car – it did not matter to me that it might rain, and I had no need of a Surtout (a great coat) for my protection against the weather. I faithfully followed the route, and found many of the original milestones, set at about ten mile intervals, still firm in the ground, but often hidden in the long autumnal grasses or set in as wall-stones. Preston to Lancaster held no surprises for me. Much of the city of Lancaster has eighteenth century buildings at its core, and the castle is still the centre of justice, with the assizes being held twice a year, but the surrounding houses have spread to create a large town.

Soon I found that corners of the route had been rounded off, and roads widened to ease the speed of car travel. In other places there were ring roads around the villages, requiring me to find the still usable original roads. Milnthorpe, as a port, was my first real surprise, for it is now several miles inland, the port having silted up when the railway bridge was built across the estuary in 1876.

The route to Kendal – if you take the old one – is not much altered and is still a mere country lane, (the 24 miles from Preston to Kendal, are only a twinkle on the modern motorway!) Kendal still retains some of its centuries old charm, for its centre is mostly organized for pedestrians, this town being totally unable to cater for vast volumes of traffic. I could find no woollen mills left or 'Kendal Cottons' for waistcoats, the old buildings having been pulled down in the late twentieth century. But smaller modern industries have grown up in the outskirts to suit modern needs.

My journey now turned towards Lake Windermere, and Isaac's destination of the village of Bowness. It is probable that he and his friend took the route via the little hamlet of Crook, for the lake is indeed about nine miles that way from Kendal as he stated. Crook is shown on the early maps, but Isaac might not have thought these groups of houses worth mentioning. His description of the endless, rocky, and rugged countryside along that route is today still a fairly accurate picture.

The town of Windermere did not exist in Isaac's time, until the railway carved a route through from Lancaster, and finally stopped at the small hamlet of Birthwaite in 1847. It went no further because of great political wrangling over the building of the hated railway, by well-known

A general purpose gig, 1870-1952. J. Finey.

146

gentry of the district in the mid 1800s. The end of the railway was known as Birthwaite Station, being the terminus of the Kendal and Windermere Junction Railway for the trains.

It soon acquired a Birthwaite Hotel, bank, shops, lodging houses, stables and horse drawn omnibuses to take the passengers down to Bowness, some three miles towards the shore of the lake. In Isaac's day, only the sheep, shepherds and the skylarks populated that area. William Wordsworth campaigned tirelessly to stop railway building and wrote a moving poem to help his cause.

Bowness is now a very busy centre for tourists, but still retains its nineteenth century charm, post-houses, pleasure boats and pier. St. Martin's Church, which the young men endowed with a wheelbarrow at midnight is still standing – since 1483! How much was built between 1831 and the mid-1870s I do not know, but the very early photographs do show many of the places that Isaac described, and accurately too, so the core of the old village still remains.

The Round House, built in 1781 for Mr. English by his neo-classical architect John Plaw, is still upon Belle Isle, and is now a tourist attraction. One of the new trades, not seen in Isaac's time, is the proliferation of cafes, and small restaurants, that cater for the thousands of present day tourists, once the sole prerogative of the inns and hotels.

The old ferryboat that was rowed across Windermere to the Ferry Inn, by two ferrymen, sank in a storm in the late1800s, but not without trace! It was lifted up from the bed of the lake in a remarkably good state of preservation in the mud, renovated, treated, and is now there for all to see at the Windermere Steamboat Museum, just outside the village to the north. The more modern ferry in 1870, following the earlier route, became a chain ferry driven by motors. It was then replaced by yet more modern engines, but still performs the same task, albeit for 21 cars – not for just one carriage, its passengers and the horses!

THE BILL OF FARE FOR CROSSING WINDERMERE, 1842

One person	2 pence
Horse and rider	4 pence
Gig with horse and passenger	1 shilling
A chaise and two horses	2 shillings
A coach and horses	3 shillings and 6 pence.

Horse drawn passengers at Birthwaite.

The original Ferry Inn burned down, and was replaced in 1870. It was the Ferry Hotel until 1948, then, in 1950, it became the Biological Station for Freshwater Fish, and recently blossomed into luxury apartments. Isaac just would not recognise all this!

But nearby, above the inn was the viewing station of Claife Heights to explore. Mr. Braithwaite built this fine house in the 1790s. Thomas West published the *First Lake District Guide Book* in 1778, describing the 'viewing of scenery' from special 'stations', and discussed seven he found around this district. In the 1830s to the 1850s, they were very fashionable for artists and early tourists.

I climbed up to the Viewing Station with great expectations, but sadly found that it had become a ruin, yet was still recognisable as the great house that it had once been. I cannot locate the date when it burned down, but I was told that in 1950 it had most of the building standing, with a very elegant Georgian staircase still intact.

I looked to the north and south, for surely the view would not have altered much, but the vast growth of trees in the intervening years have taken their toll on what could be viewed now, hiding houses amongst the trees, and the wicker gate and paths are covered with brambles and bracken.

Many of the large private houses situated on the lakeside (such as Storrs Hall, built by Col. John Bolton, a West Indian Merchant, who died in 1837), were built by the new cotton mill owners, sugar refiners, captains of shipping, and other growing industrialists in Lancashire and Liverpool, their businesses often based on slave trading. These large establishments have survived, but serve very different purposes today. Built in the late 1700s and early 1800s, they are now mostly hotels, youth hostels, or establishments for water based and mountain sports. By 1787 there began movements to be rid of slave trading, and the two Acts of Abolition of Slavery in 1807 and 1833 saw the end of this terrible trade.

My journey to Hawkshead made up for my disappointments, for here was an almost unaltered piece of the journey – at least until arriving at Hawkshead! Esthwaite Water was as serene and untroubled a lake as Isaac had found it with several islands seemingly floating upon its surface. White houses still are dotted around its edge amongst the farmlands, and Hawkshead in the distance looked inviting.

The viewing station, Claife Heights, 1981.

Hawkshead excludes motor traffic luckily, to a nearby car park, for I found that the town is almost exactly as it once was; the Red Lion, still in business as an inn, offered me photographs of 150-year-old views. The old grammar school was founded in 1585, the dilapidated sight of which caused so much surprise to Isaac, has now been well preserved to house a museum of its local history. William Wordsworth studied there. Its rise and fall as an academic establishment was well documented, with Dr. D. B. Hickie LLD (headmaster 1829-1862) listed as one of its noted schoolmasters.

The curator of this establishment kindly allowed me to photograph some of the ancient paintings, showing a bygone view of this village, and gave me permission to use them in my book. Upon enquiring where I could find the Hawkshead Courthouse attached to a medieval manorial farm, that was once held by Furness Abbey (dissolved in 1537), and since 1932 owned by the National Trust, I soon spotted it across a field, for it is now being used for out-buildings beside a farm. Hawkshead Church has now been cleaned of its white shell of the eighteenth century, and is returned to its former Lakeland stone of previous years, standing with a commanding view upon the hill like a small fortress.

Transporting a parcel for Mr Clarke from Preston to Hawkshead, saved

The old ferryboat, now at the Windermere Steamboat Museum.

this object from an expensive post-coach journey! William Dockra started a postal service in towns in 1680, but by 1801 the one-penny post had increased to two pence per ounce weight. This was to help to finance the Napoleonic War. But it was all overhauled again by Rowland Hill, who by 10 January 1840 introduced a one penny stamp for all, with a not very successful glue upon its rear side. By then there were more frequent post-coaches for transportation to wider destinations.

My travels next took me along the almost unfrequented and unchanged route to Ambleside, winding amongst the farmlands and following the contours of the northern part of Windermere. This area has been bypassed by the traffic that prefers another better-developed and widened route. I soon reached the Low Wood Hotel, still in business, but enlarged and extended almost beyond recognition, with a water sports centre and marina for a variety of craft along its waterfront – but the views and the setting in the landscape are still the same!

The comment by Mary at the Low Wood Hotel about taxes on dogs brings forth a short explanation. There were several strange taxes in the early 1800s. The French Revolution (1790) and the subsequent war with France (1793-1801) was expensive, so one of these taxes was on keeping dogs; the Act of Repeal in 1822 altered it to a, "Person having One Exempted Dog, all others being paid for, apart from the exempted groups (Hounds, Greyhounds, Working Curs – *sheepdogs* - Pointers, Terriers and Lurchers)." Licences lapsed through time and were finally abolished in 1987!

The tollgates attached to the tollhouses are worthy of note, for these usually eight-sided houses are still to be found in many places. (I have seen eight, and one is at the beginning of Ambleside.) The tollgate system was taken over by Westmorland County Council in 1899 that then nurtured the increasing road system with improved surfaces. A Scottish engineer, John Loudon McAdam, (1756-1836) who worked for the Bristol Turnpike Trust in the early 1800s revolutionised the road building methods, and by 1830, McAdam roads were much in evidence throughout the country, especially the main routes, but this did not pertain to the many minor ones, not owned by the county councils, until late in the twentieth century!

I have been in Ambleside many times, but on this occasion my visit was but a short one, for the town was too busy with vehicles and people to linger long. Its core of eighteenth century narrow streets and buildings are delightful to

The village of Rydal.

meander around, if you have the time to find them.

Use your imagination to transport yourself back two centuries, ignoring the layer of twenty first century advertising trash, trendy tea parlours and traffic wardens! Very early on a cold day in midweek January will suffice to give you a better feel of still being in 1831, for it is all there!

Rydal Water and Grasmere are likewise still there in almost original form. Rydal Water is so enclosed by the surrounding hills that the surface of the water hardly feels a breath of stirring air, giving the lake the appearance of a giant mirror laid to rest on a green table.

These small towns did not alter much for a hundred years. The National Trust, started in 1884, then took a hand in events in the mid 1900s, and together with the National Parks Authority (1951), made the preservation of Lake District villages and buildings more certain for another century.

I went with a friend to pay a visit to the Swan Inn on the outskirts of Grasmere; indeed it is still there, and at first glance, perhaps, not much altered from its coaching days. Not so the modernised interior, and when we stopped for a little refreshment there, we remembered the situation of Isaac and his companions so long ago who chose to underpay the, 'What you please' servants.

The road going north is at the start of Dunmail Raise, and this part of the journey is the most alien road to this story. The etching in the book shows that all the gentlemen had to disembark at the foot of the mountain, to lighten the load for the horses pulling the coach and walk to the top, where they waited; sometimes they had to assist pushing as well! Isaac's party had light gigs, but would still get down on steep parts to assist their horses.

The new lake of Thirlmere was created in 1894 by the Manchester City Corporation, which had bought Wythburn and Leathes Water in 1889, and flooded these two lakes together with the village of Armboth, and other buildings and farms, to create a very much larger reservoir named Thirlmere. Sadly the Cherry Tree Inn, and the road upon which it stood are now gone for ever.

Thus I travelled, not amongst the boulders and possible footpads of former years up this notorious route, but upon a somewhat flattened, widened and less curvaceous route. King Dunmail's gravestones *could* be the pile set between the dual carriageway area upon the crown of this hill, but it is difficult to ascertain now.

I travelled along the side of Thirlmere, a sanitised route, shrouded with trees hiding glimpses of the high fells around. Thence I travelled through St. Johns Vale, which part seemed very little altered, and eventually down a steep bank into Keswick.

History has shown that Keswick owed its prosperity to the mineral mining all over Cumberland and Westmorland from Henry III's time in the 1500s, to the cannon balls of the 1800s. Also, Queen Elizabeth I needed much copper for arms and strengthening warships. German miners were brought in for their skills in the eighteenth century, and black lead graphite was in great demand to be used in armaments.

The mining of silver and gold also made the area an important one, and much of the population was involved in the mining industry. So when Isaac's friend discussed the mining of this area, he knew very little of the total truth, and its subsequent influences.

My next port of call was the Queen's Head, but my first glance at this large building facing the square of Keswick, showed it to be a grand Victorian edifice. I enquired within as to how long this hotel had been there, and whether it was on the site of an earlier Queen's Head? I was soon informed of the truth.

"Gang down yon ginnel aside t'hotel, and tha'll see t'ould lyle Queen's 'Ead. We use it as tha games room - snooker and t' like."

What a change of use for the old inn! But this building was the original and its interior showed the original bar and old benches!

I did not take a sail upon the lake, set amongst the unchanging mountain ranges, but drove along the western side of Derwentwater until I reached the Lodore Hotel at its far end. This building has changed its name according to changing owners over the years, but it was obviously another Victorian building at its main core.

Asking similar questions as in Keswick, the staff showed me old

The old Queen's Head, Keswick.

photographs that were lining their walls of the 'new Lodore' when built in 1870 – but the exciting thing was that the Stephenson's Inn was still there *beside* the new building, used as a coaching halt. It was mentioned in *A Forthright Ramble to the Lakes* in 1795, Thomas Mossop being the proprietor. I asked for and obtained permission to use a picture of the Stephenson's Inn, reproduced earlier in this book. The Lodore Falls lacked much water after a very dry summer, so my experience of the place fell short of the extreme excitement, as Isaac experienced it, yet it was still an impressive sight.

The discussions about the sad fate of James Radcliffe, Earl of Derwentwater, who was executed in 1716 for supporting the Jacobites, alerted me to finding out about the Greenwich Hospital. This was started in 1696 the driving force being King William III as a tribute to his dear wife Mary II, who died of smallpox in 1694. She had agitated for such a project during her lifetime.

The Royal Hospital for Seamen, was 'A refuge for all,' and was funded by various bequests, prize money from many enemy ships captured in the eighteenth century and other confiscations by the crown. After the execution of Captain Kidd for piracy his vast treasure was forfeited, to swell the hospital coffers, and, in 1735 George II gave all the vast wealth and mineral rights to them from the Derwentwater estates. It became first the Royal Naval College, which moved to a more suitable building, and is now the National Maritime Museum.

Having reached the ultimate point of this journey, I retraced my steps through Keswick, St. John's Vale, and thence to Thirlmere. Helvellyn loomed large into the swirling crown of clouds, and brought to mind the sad story of Charles Gouch, a Quaker from Kendal, who lost his life in 1805. At this point there is a memorial erected in 1890 to the man and faithful hound, organised by Canon Rawnsley of Crosthwaite; thus the past is recorded for 'future generations to ponder.'

If you care to climb up there, you may gaze upon its old, chiselled surface. Upon this stone is written:

"Beneath this spot were found in 1805
The remains of Charles Gough, killed by a fall from the rocks,
& His dog was still guarding the skeleton.
Sir Walter Scott describes the event in his poem
'The dark brow of the mighty Helvellyn'
Wordsworth records it in his lines on Fidelity
In memory of that Love and Strength of feeling
This stone is erected, 1890."

Concerning the painter, William Westall, whom Isaac and his friend Yates met, I discovered that this fine artist, originally from Hartford, was a botanical painter originally. When he was nineteen, he joined the *HMS Investigator* as the recording artist for the expedition, and then spent many years in Australia. He became quite well known as an exhibitor there and in England, and was

The church at Ings, 1989.   W. M. Stuart.

155

made an associate of the RA. He first went to visit the Lake District in 1811, subsequently spending many winters roaming the area for landscape painting, and became good friends with Wordsworth and Southey, and many others whom he met on his travels, including Isaac.

I continued to retrace my steps, following as near as possible the route that Isaac took past Troutbeck, Ings and Staveley, there watching the timeless quality of the torrents tumbling down the River Kent without end. It was worth a lingering visit, to muse about the natural forces still there, for Isaac and his friends, and then for me.

William Westall ARA, 1781-1850. A pencil and watercolour portrait, painted in 1845 by his son, Robert Westall.

I travelled on again to Kendal, but here it is now a modern route. One needs to deviate along the old roads, to visit places, which still have their original cores. It made me feel that the modern trunk routes, chosen to avoid the villages, have in fact preserved them for posterity. I followed the old coastal route to Lancaster, over the River Lune, then finally returned to Preston.

The pleasure and anticipation with which Isaac set off on his totally unknown journey, one which I tried to recreate, gives me much food for thought. He viewed all he saw with eighteenth and early nineteenth century eyes and knowledge.

Therefore I have had to ask many historical questions to place myself back into the thoughts of a person living in 1831. Isaac's method of travel with a horse and gig allowed him time to regard, and mentally record, infinitely more than I could ever do in a modern vehicle, so it has been a pleasure to take my time, stop, look, be nosey, ask questions, and use my imagination, to recreate this earlier era.

I hope any reader of this book will enjoy doing the same.

Time to blow the candle out.

Paintings, photographs and illustrations, listed by letter

LETTER 1

Preston, from Penwortham Hill.	Etching.	J. Harwood	1832
'We proceeded to Lancaster in better spirits'	Pen drawing	W. M. Stuart	1980
The County Boundary Stone	Pen sketch	W. M. Stuart	2005
'The Tea Party'	Watercolour	W. M. Stuart	2005
Milnthorpe Sands	Etching	T. Allom	1834
A sketch of the Port of Milnthorpe	Pen sketch	Anon	1835
The Commercial Hotel, Kendal	Photograph	Fenty's collection	1860

LETTER 2

The main street, Kendal	Etching	W. Westall A.R.A.	1828
'Visiting The Woollen Mills'	Paint/pen	W. M. Stuart	1990
From Kendal Castle, looking at the town	Etching	T. Allom	1833
Topcoats and frock coats	Pen drawing	Fashion magazine	1829

LETTER 3

Bowness and Windermere Lake	Etching	T. Allom	1833
The White Lion Hotel, Bowness	Photograph	Fenty's collection	1860
Bowness Bay, Windermere	Pencil sketch	Isaac Simpson	1831
'A young man of some fortune'	Pen sketch	W. M. Stuart	1990
The village of Bowness	Photograph	Fenty's collection	1860
Bowness Church	Photograph	Fenty's collection	1860
The Crown Inn	Photograph	Fenty's collection	1860

LETTER 4

Bowness from Belle Isle, Windermere	Etching	T. Allom	1832
Bowness, facing Windermere	Etching	J. Harwood	1842
Bowness Bay, Windermere	Old painting	Fenty's collection	1795
Storrs Hall, from the road to Ulverston	Etching	W. Banks	1832
Windermere, looking north	Watercolour	W. M. Stuart	1994

LETTER 5

The Round House, Belle Isle	Watercolour	W. M. Stuart	1997
The Viewing Station	Etching	J. Walton	1832
Windermere from the Station	Old painting	Anon	1800

LETTER 6

The Ferry House Inn	Photograph	Fenty's collection	1856
'The Northumbria' steam engine	Pen drawing	W. M. Stuart	1982
'Some of the small islands'	Watercolour	W. M. Stuart	1997
'Loading the ferry with horse and cart'	Photograph	Fenty's collection	1860
Windermere Lake from Ferry House	Etching	T. Allom	1833
Looking down on Esthwaite Water	Photograph	W. M. Stuart	2005

LETTER 7

Hawkshead – painting on wood	Oil painting	In School Museum	1790
Hawkshead Church – detail of painting	Oil painting	In School Museum	1790
Ruins of the old monastery	Photograph	W. M. Stuart	1987
Hawkshead Seminary – detail of painting	Oil painting	In School Museum	1790
Coniston stage coach by the Red Lion	Photograph	In the Red Lion	1845
'Watching the Harvest gatherers'	Pen drawing	W. M. Stuart	1992
The Head of Windermere	Photograph	Fenty's collection	1860
'We did all we could to overtake the Curricle'	Pen drawing	W. M. Stuart	1982
Details of the LowWood Hotel	Etching	W. Banks	1825
Yates, my friend	Pencil drawing	Isaac Simpson	1830
The Low Wood Inn on Windermere	Etching	W. Banks	1825

LETTER 8

Head of Windermere Lake	Etching	G. Pickering	1835
Lakers at the head of Lake Windermere	Pen drawing	W. M. Stuart	1985
'A great number of dogs at Low Wood'	Etching detail	T. Allom	1834
The Toll Gate at Waterhead, Ambleside	Photograph	Fenty's collection	1860
Rydal Hall, the seat of Lady Fleming	Photograph	W. M. Stuart	1980
Langdale Pikes, near Rydal	Water painting	W. M. Stuart	2005

LETTER 9

Rydal Mount, the seat of Wordsworth	Photograph	W. M. Stuart	1989
The Upper Falls, Rydal Mount	Etching	H. Gastineau	1833
The Lower Falls, Rydal Mount	Etching	G. Pickering	1833

LETTER 10

Ambleside, Westmorland, 1830	Pen drawing	W. M. Stuart	1989
The approach to Ambleside.	Etching	T. Allom	1834
The Bridge House, Ambleside	Etching	T. Allom	1834
William Wordsworth	Pencil sketch	W. M. Stuart	1980
Rydal Water	Photograph	Fenty's collection	1850
Grasmere	Watercolour	Isaac Simpson	1831
The Swan Inn, Ambleside	Photograph	W. M. Stuart	1995

LETTER 11

Dunmail Raise	Etching	J. Harwood	1830
Cherry Tree Inn	Photograph	Fenty's collection	1885
'Crosthwaite started off on his mare…'	Pen drawing	W. M. Stuart	1977
Wythburn or Leathes Water	Etching	G. Pickering	1833
'We now approached the isolated building'	Painting	W. M. Stuart	1989

LETTER 12

Vale of St. John and Saddleback	Etching	G. Pickering	1835
'Equipped with Lanthorn in hand, we set off'	Pen drawing	W. M. Stuart	2002
Where the spirits of the Druids live	Painting	W. M. Stuart	1994
Keswick from the Ambleside Road	Etching	S. Bough	1840

PAINTINGS, PHOTOGRAPHS AND ILLUSTRATIONS

LETTER 13

Keswick from Greta Bridge	Etching	H. Castineau	1833
Keswick Lake from Barrow Common	Etching	W. Westall, A.R.A.	1820
Lower Market Street, Keswick	Pen drawing	W. M. Stuart	1992
Greta Hall, Southey's house	Pencil drawing	W. M. Stuart	1992
The standing stones, Castlerigg	Painting	W. M. Stuart	1985
The islands upon Derwentwater	Etching detail	T. Allom	1832

LETTER 14

Derwentwater, from Castle Head	Etching	T. Allom	1832
Derwentwater, from Vickers Island	Etching	W. Bellers	1840
Keswick Lake	Etching	J. M. W. Turner, R.A.	1837
The Lodore Waterfall	Etching	J. Farington	1816
Mountains south of Derwentwater	Etching detail	T. Allom	1832

LETTER 15

Stephenson's Arms, Derwentwater	Photograph	From Lodore Hotel	1848
View of Derwentwater from above the falls	Etching	W. Westall, A.R.A.	1819
The Cataract at Lodore	Etching	T. Allom	1833
Skiddaw in the sunset	Etching	P. J. Loutherbourg	1787
View near Keswick	Etching	F. Wheatly	1787

LETTER 16

Greta Hall and Keswick Bridge	Etching	W. Westall, A.R.A.	1835
'The Artist walked alongside of us…'	Pen drawing	W. M. Stuart	2005
St John's Vale, Cumberland	Photograph	W. M. Stuart	1997
Thirlmere and Helvellyn, looking south	Etching	T. Allom	1833
'Streamlets running down the ravines'	Watercolour	W. M. Stuart	1991
Leathes Water or Wythburn Water	Etching	G. Pickering	1833

LETTER 17

Staveley, Westmorland	Pencil drawing	W. M. Stuart	1860
Bridge over River Kent, Kendal (detail)	Etching	T. Allom	1833
'Bargaining for a pony'	Pen drawing	W. M. Stuart	2007
Preston, Lancashire	Etching	J. Walker	1790

EPILOGUE

General purpose Gig	Photograph	J. Finney	1928
Passengers on their way to Bowness	Photograph	Fenty's collection	1870
Viewing Station	Photograph	W. M. Stuart	1979
The old Ferry boat	Photograph	W. M. Stuart	1979
Village of Rydal	Photograph	W. M. Stuart	2000
The Old Queen's Head	Photograph	W. M. Stuart	2000
The Church at Ings	Painting	W. M. Stuart	1989
William Westall ARA,	Watercolour	Robert Westall.	1845

Etched illustrations

(List of eighteenth and nineteenth century etchings, artists and the engravers)

PLACE	ARTIST	ENGRAVER	DATE
Preston, from Penwortham Hill, Lancs.	J. Harwood	R. Winkles	1832
Milnthorpe Sands, Westmorland	T. Allom	J. Tingle	1832
Kendal, the Main Street, Westmorland	W. Westall A.R.A.	S. Rawle	1828
The Bridge at Kendal, Westmorland	T. Allom	W. Le Petit	1833
Kendal, from the Castle, Westmorland	T. Allom	W. Le Petit	1833
In Bowness, facing Lake Windermere	J. Harwood	F. Harwood	1842
Bowness and Windermere Lake	T. Allom	W. Le Pitit	1833
Bowness, from Belle Isle, Windermere	T. Allom	J. Redaway	1832
Windermere from Road to Ulverston	W. Banks, Edinburgh	W. Banks	1832
Windermere from Low Wood Hotel	W. Banks, Edinburgh	W. Bank	1832
Head of Windermere Lake	G. Pickering	W. Le Petit	1835
The Viewing Station, Windermere, Lancs.	J. Walton	J. Walton	1832
Windermere Lake, from Ferry House	T. Allom	W. Taylor	1833
The Low Wood Hotel on Windermere	W. Banks, Edinburgh	W. Banks	1825
The Lower Falls at Rydal, Westmorland	G. Pickering	W. Le Petit	1833
The Upper Falls at Rydal, Westmorland	H. Gastineau	T. Jeavons	1833
Approach to Ambleside, Westmorland	T. Allom	T. Jeavons	1834
Bridge House, Ambleside, Westmorland	T. Allom	T. Jeavons	1834
Dunmail Raise, Cumberland	J. Harwood	F. Harwood	1830
Thirlmere Bridge, looking north	T. Allom	W. Le Petit	1833
Thirlmere, or Wythburn Water, Cumberland	G. Pickering	W. Le Petit	1833
The Vale of St. John and Saddleback	G. Pickering	M. J. Starling	1835
Keswick, from the Ambleside Road	S. Bough	W. H. Lizars	1840
Keswick from Greta Bridge, Cumberland	H. Castineau	W. Le Petit	1833
Keswick Lake from Barrow Common	W. Westall, A.R.A;	W. Westall	1820
View of Derwentwater from Vickers Island	W. Bellers	W. H. Lizars	1840
The Lodore Waterfall	J. Farington, A.R.A;	J. Landseer	1816
The Lodore Cataract, Cumberland	T. Allom	J. C. Bentley	1833
Derwent Water from Castle Head	T. Allom	S. Lacey	1832
Greta Hall from Keswick Bridge	W. Westall, A.R.A;	E. Francis	1835
Thirlmere from Raven Crag, Cumberland	W. Banks	W. Banks	1832
Thirlmere and Helvellyn looking south	T. Allom	W. Le Petit	1833
Preston and the itinerant, Lancashire	W. Orme	J. Walker	1790

Glossary of unusual words in the 21st century which were common in 1831

ORIGINAL WORD	MEANING	EXTRA MEANINGS
Accession	Accumulation	Attainment
Acclivity	Ascent	The upward slope
Amatory	Expressing love	Designed to excite love
Anchorite	Recluse	One who has withdrawn from the world
Antiquarian	Ancient studies	Collecting of antiques
Apocryphal	Uncertain	Of doubtful authenticity
Appraise	To make value judgement	Estimate the worth of
Aprise	To tell	To indicate
Assiduous	Diligent	Devoted
Benighted	Stranded at night	Left in a dark place
Brogue	Broad accent; strong shoe	North country or Irish accent
Cabalistic	Concealed	A mystic, or occultist
Cantabs	Students	Undergraduates from Cambridge
Carking	Burdensome	Worrying
Cataract	Waterfall	Immense flow of water
Cicerone	Guide who explains	(Cicero = Roman orator)
Cimmirian	Gloomy	Thick
Cornrick	Method of storing corn	Like a haystack (rick = stack)
Cot	Small house	Cottage (old English)
Coxcomb	Conceited	Upstart
Cumberland	Fellow countryman	From Combrogie (old Welsh)
Debark	Arrive, get off	Get down from
Declivity	Downward slope	Descending slope of a hill
Dejeuner	Special meal	(French = have lunch)
Demesne	Territory	Estate, domain
Descant	Talk at large	Hold forth
Encomium	Praise	Formal, high flown praise (Greek)
Epicurus	Self Indulgence	From the Greek philosopher = Epicurus
Epithet	Expressing quality	Appellation attributes
Evince	Indicate	To show plainly, to conquer
Forage	To feed a horse	Food for horses or cattle
Garrulous	Talkative	Continual tedious talking
Gawks	Clumsy and awkward	To gawk = to stare stupidly
Gig	Two Wheeled Carriage	One or two seater, drawn by one horse

Grandiloquent	High flown words	Fancy language
Heptarchy	7 kingdoms of Angles and Saxons	
Hick	Rustic; Rushes;	Countrified manners, speech or dress
Hightly	Named	Called (O.E. = heht = to name)
His Majesty	William IV 1830-1837	A tax was paid to the Crown on most dogs from 1822
Hostler	Ostler	Inn servant in charge of horses and stables
Ignis Fatuus	Will o' the wisp	Light flitting over marshes; phosphorescent
Immolated	Sacrificed	To kill as a sacrifice
Instanter	Immediately	Without an instant's delay
Interpose	Interject remark	Intervene
Itinerants	Travellers	Gypsies
Lanthorn	An old lantern	Light
Laudatory	Praiseworthy	To praise or celebrate
Loquacity	Talkativeness	Having a great deal to say
Lord Brougham	Lord Chancellor 1831	Gave his name to a two horse carriage
Manufactory	Place for making goods	Factory
Mecum et Tecum	Mine and Thine	Mecum et Tecum (Latin - mine & yours)
Meet	Expedient	Appropriate, suitable
Mendicant	Beggar	Depending on alms for a living
Mettled	Courageous, spirited	Having endurance
Morpheus	Sleep	Morpheus = Greek God of Dreams
Peculiarly	Singularly	Odd, strange
Pellucid	Translucent	Clear, limpid
Peregrination	Journey	Travelling through or along
Peremptory	Dictatorial	Bossy, dogmatic
Potations	Beverages	Suitable for drinking (Latin - Potaire - drink)
Prepossessing	Attractive	Favourable impression from the start
Procrastination	Postponing action	Being dilatory
Propinquity	Nearness in place or time	Kinship
Quantum Suffict	Enough quantity	Satisfying amount
Redounds	Comes back	Recoil upon
Rencontre	Skirmish	Casual meeting
Requite	Repay	Return, give back
Retinue	A group of people	People usually in some stated order
Rhetoric	Eloquence	The use of language
Sanguinary	Bloodthirsty	Cruel, inhuman
Sate	O.E. past and p.p. of sit	Sat down
Satellite	Henchman or hanger-on	Servant (French, Latin = Satelles)

GLOSSARY

Sequestered	Isolated, secluded	Set apart
Shewed	O.E. for showed	Alternative spelling – shewing = showing
Shilling	Old coinage of England	12 pennies = 1 shilling; 20 shillings = £1
Somerset	O.E. for Somersault	Turn upside down
Sonorousness	Rich sound, resonant	Powerful sound
Station	Observatory	Viewing station
Stept	O.E. for stepped	To walk
Sublunary	Earthly	Terrestrial
Surtout	Overcoat	Great-coat for horse-riding (O.Fr- over all)
Tartarean	Savage person	Wild unkempt man
Thraldom	Dependence	Enslavement
Toper	Drinker	Habitual drinker, sot
Umbrage	Shade	Shadow cast by trees
Unhippingly	Not depressing	(Hipping = depressing)
Usuary	Interest earned on money	Getting out more than put in
Verdant	Green and fresh	(Verdure = greenery)
Verge	Edge	Border
Vernal	Of spring	Appropriate to youth or spring like
Vicissitudes	Changes of fortune	Ups and downs, change of seasons
Vociferate	Shout, clamour	Speak harshly, loudly, insistently
Vulcan	Old name for blacksmith	Greek God of fire and smiths
Westmorland	Part of Cumbria now	Westmorland and Cumberland amalgamated in 1974
Wherewith	Substance	i.e. money or food needed
Will-o-the-wisp	Ignited marsh gasses	Ignis Fatuus
Woodbine	Honeysuckle	Climbing perfumed flowering plant

Bibliography

Simpson: Records of an ancient yeoman family of the W. Riding of Yorkshire, 1544-1922, Col. Stephen Simpson, TD, DL.

History of the Firm of Stephen Simpson, Col. Stephen Simpson, TD, DL.

English Economic History, George W. Southgate, BA

Social & Economic History of Britain 1760-1965, Pauline Gregg, PhD, B.Sc.

Images of Westmorland, John Marsh

Regional history of railways - The Lake Counties, David Joy

Wordsworth's Lakeland, John Marsh and John Garbutt

First Lake District Guide Book, 1778, Thomas West

The Tourists New Guide, 1819, William Green

A Forthright Ramble to the Lakes, Budworth

Concise Description of the English Lakes, 1825, Jonathan Otley

Handbook to the Lakes, 1854, James Gibson of Ambleside

The District of the Lakes, 1818, Jonathan Otley

Chambers Dictionary, 1901, W & R Chambers, Edinburgh

Websters Dictionary, 1890 (American version of Early English)